TOUCHING THE EARTH

Roberta Bondar

KEY PORTER BOOKS

This book is dedicated to my mother, Mildred, and my father, Edward, who always believed that I would fly in space. Their love of the outdoors and photography have made my world a wonderful place to explore.

Canadian Cataloguing in Publication Data

Bondar, Roberta Lynn, 1945 -

    Touching the earth

Includes bibliographical references and index.

ISBN 1-55013-575-9

1. Bondar, Roberta Lynn, 1945-   .   2. Discovery (Spacecraft).   3. Space shuttles.   4. Earth. 5. Women astronauts - Canada - Biography. I. Title

TL789.85.B66A3 1994   629.45'0092   C94-931217-7

Key Porter Books Limited

70 The Esplanade

Toronto, Ontario

Canada M5E 1R2

The publisher gratefully acknowledges the assistance of the Canada Council, the Department of Communications, the Ontario Publishing Centre and the Ontario Arts Council in the publication of this work.

Design and page composition: Peter Maher

Printed on recycled, acid-free paper

Printed and bound in Canada

94 95 96 97 98 6 5 4 3 2 1

ACKNOWLEDGEMENTS

After my space flight, I was encouraged by my family, friends, and professional colleagues to describe what I saw and felt while I was floating above them in January 1992. This appealed to me, especially when Anna Porter believed that it was a good idea. Of course, my mom, a retired teacher, was right there when I asked her to review the draft manuscript. Her thoughtful suggestions and many hours of filtering my written thoughts enriched the text. My sister, Barbara, a professional writer, never hesitated to give me advice, both written and verbal. My close friends provided support, accurate information, and critiques throughout the many months of researching and writing the manuscript, and so I gratefully thank Robyn Young, Flo Stein, and Betty Roots.

Several outstanding resource people facilitated my gaining access to the photographic record of the United States Space Program: NASA employees and contractors who work for NASA, Johnson Space Center, Houston, Texas — Building 424, Barry Schroder (R.M.S.); Building 2, Becky Fryday (Media Services Corp.); Building 31, Dr. Michael Helfert (NASA), Patricia Jaklitch (Hernandez Engineering Inc.), Dr. Kam Lulla; Building 4, Jude Alexander (Rockwell), Dot Davis (NASA Retired); Building 4N, Sharon Jones (Rockwell) and Karin Porter (Rockwell). I would also like to thank Mary Noel Black of the Lunar and Planetary Institute; Dr. Alfred C. Coats, Lisa M. Reed, and Jack Sevier of the Universities Space Research Association; Amelia Budge and Laura Gleasner of the Earth Data Analysis Center, Albuquerque, New Mexico; STS-42 staff and trainers at JSC, KSC, MSFC, ARC, and the flight crew of STS-42, especially my Earth-viewing pals, Ron, Steve, and Bill. Without the commitment of the following agencies, IML-1 would not have happened: National Aeronautics Space Administration (NASA), the European Space Agency (ESA), the Canadian Space Agency (CSA), the French National Center for Space Studies (CNES), the German Space Agency, the German Aerospace Research Establishment (DARA/DLR), and the National Space Development Agency of Japan (NASDA).

Telephone, typing expertise, and library search assistance were most amiably and professionally performed by Rosemary Viola and Cindy McClung. Laurie Coulter persevered through deadlines and faxlines to help produce a book that reflects my around-the-world view from both space and the outer crust of the Earth.

Photography Acknowledgements

Edward Bondar: 10, 13; Roberta Bondar: 43 (inset), 44 (right below), 63, 64, 65, 67 (inset), 71 (inset), 83 (inset), 89, 92 (right), 95 (inset), 97 (inset), 99 (inset), 109 (inset), 109 (right), 112, 113 (right), 115, 116 (right), 117, 118, 120, 125 (inset), 127 (right), 131; JPL/NASA: 16, 83 (left), 137 (right), 139 (left above), 139 (left below), 139 (right); NASA: 1, 2, 6, 21, 25, 28, 31, 33, 39, 40, 43 (left), 44 (left), 44 (right above), 46, 51, 54, 57, 58, 61, 66, 67 (left), 69, 70, 71 (left), 73, 75, 77, 85, 92 (left), 95 (left), 95 (right), 97 (left), 97 (right), 99 (left), 100, 101, 103, 109 (left), 113 (left), 116 (left), 116 (inset), 122, 125 (left), 127 (left); Betty Roots: 79; Flo Stein: 9; U.S. Geological Survey, Flagstaff, Arizona: 137 (left)

C O N T E N T S

L I F T O F F !

WAITING FOR THE COUNTDOWN CLOCK to resume, it's hard not to be impatient, especially with all this gear on. I can't look out the mid-deck window because it's covered on entry and reentry with a metal shield. I can't read a book in the eerie green light of the chemsticks, and my orange pressure gloves make it impossible to push the buttons on my microcassette recorder without fear of dropping it onto the cold steel floor. Retrieving it, or anything else that gravity traps in the darkness, is out of the question; the six other crew members and I are all locked in place on our backs with lap belts and connectors, which will prevent us from smashing into the floor during the ride "uphill." My helmet, secured onto the neck ring of the space suit by "dog teeth," seems overly large for my head. Its rigidity somewhat restricts my neck motion. Although I feel like a goldfish with an anchor, I welcome the luxury of time to think about my preparation for this moment. It's a comfort to reflect back and recall as much detail as possible, to keep my memory hot for the adventure ahead.

If I had viewed a film clip of this scene when I was eight years old, would I have believed it? Perhaps. The seeds of space exploration had been sown at an early age. Come to think of it, I spent all my free time dreaming about space, wondering how I would pull it off, never willing to give up on what I felt was my destiny. Every birthday, I asked for a plastic model-rocket kit, a chemistry set, or a doctor's bag. I had to wait three more weeks until Christmas for the hockey sticks, Meccano sets, or basketball equipment. Not that *Discovery* looks anything like those early model rockets, which kept me wrapped up in my personal dream of becoming a space explorer. Real spacecraft use bolts, special glass, and computers. So far, the "glue" looks better on the real thing.

I remember my first space helmet. It was 1953. The excitement mounted, even then, as my sister Barbara and I waited for the chewing gum company to send the space headgear we had ordered. "They'll arrive in a large box because they'll have an air hose and a glass cover," I thought. The long-awaited day finally arrived. The postman came to the door with two flat brown envelopes in his weathered hands, one for each of us. I was running upstairs to check out my moon rocket plans when Mom called out, "Girls, they're here!" What, squashed up in those envelopes? I was a logical child and "flat" was not associated in my mind with a space helmet. However, big sisters have more knowledge about such things. "Let's put them on and go exploring," Barbara suggested with great enthusiasm.

The cardboard helmets were tall, rectangular, and white. Although they had no glass, each had a large square opening so that I could scratch my nose and eat — two activities that are impossible to do with the visor down and locked on the NASA launch/entry suit. The Dubble Bubble helmets were also much lighter and sat comfortably on the shoulders, dropping rakishly over the front and back. We two

From an early age, I was fascinated with outer space and spent many hours putting together plastic models of airplanes, rockets, satellites, and space stations.

intrepid space heroes set forth on our first mission in proper gear, complete with one red and one green Flash-Gordon-style water pistol and enough provisions for the exploration of the planet bounded by McGregor Avenue, Edward's Lane, and Upton Road in Sault Ste. Marie, Ontario.

In those days, I assumed I was already trained in everything that was needed for space flight. After all, what science-fiction movie or book even mentioned training? I made up my own operational techniques because no one else understood the intricate workings of the pieces of painted plywood that were my spacecraft. I was trainer and trainee. I was commander and crew.

Now, however, on this, my first real space mission, I am Payload Specialist One (PS1), science detail, on the first flight of the International Microgravity Laboratory Mission (IML-1). I represent Canada on this international crew. In preparation for this moment, I've spent five years of high school, eighteen years of university, eight years in the Canadian Astronaut Program, and three years of book work and practice dedicated to this flight. I've studied science for the mission in Europe and North America so that I will be able to perform inflight experiments for scientists all over the world, and for a year I've practised how to live in the shuttle with my fellow crew members. But although I know I'm well trained and fit to fly, no one really feels prepared for space flight. Travelling at twenty-five times the speed of sound is a mental boundary as well as a physiological one, which astronauts can only experience once they are in space.

But years before all that formal training, I was hungry for this day. My preparation for space flight continued throughout my preadolescent and adolescent years. An uncle's gift of a crystal set each for Barbara and me added a tremendous level of fidelity to an earlier system of plastic toy radio receivers and wires. My parents helped us develop various life skills through camping and activities in church groups, the family YMCA, and Girl Guides of Canada. (They also practised survival training during this time, especially at bedtime as they negotiated their way around our space station to say goodnight.)

In those days it was fun to explore the surface of a pretend planet or asteroid, to look for specimens of plants and soil, and to make contact with a strange new life-form — usually an unsuspecting neighbour. We moved rapidly into the era of space photography with our Brownie cameras, which we were never without. "You have to document everything," instructed my sister. I nodded my head in the most knowing way possible. But black and white? How could I take black-and-white pictures of a planet and make it look real? Fortunately, my View-Master provided colour images. Its reels gave me my first training in planet observation. The "canals" and red soil of Mars, spaceship interiors, stars, the moon, aliens — they were right there on film whenever I wanted them.

On Sunday trips to the shores of Lake Superior, the family car became more crowded after I insisted on bringing all my space equipment along. By day, the trip was enchanting. By night, the stars were always there over the lake, beckoning me to leave my own planet. The trip home was filled with sleep and dreams of the next day's adventures and observations. Life was fascinating and very, very

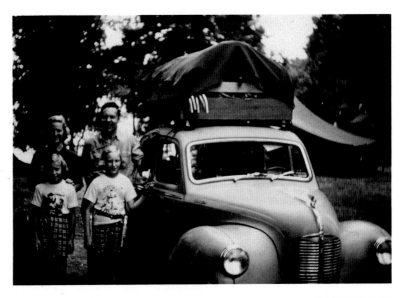

My family enjoyed camping, particularly on the shores of Lake Superior.

big. It was too much for one small explorer to record on film all by herself.

I have always had a great interest in both adventure and photography. Even when I was a child, I sensed that photography captures history. At home, "Saturday night at the movies" consisted of family fun preserved forever on standard 8-mm film and 35-mm slides. Some family members preferred the action of the movies, but I thought the slides were clearer and more colourful. It was never a hardship to set up the equipment for those wonderful evenings. As an adult, I developed a deep respect for the technological side of photography — the sharpness of an image, the contrast between light and shadow, and the potential of the equipment itself.

I had to wait until 1984 to see photographs of Earth observation from space. During astronaut training, I was able to watch the hundreds of photographs taken on shuttle flights projected onto a large screen. It was as though I had been suddenly transported back into the childhood world of my View-Master, but instead of drawings or cartoons, now I was seeing the real thing. "How did they do that?" frequently spilled into my conscious thoughts. My knowledge of viewing the Earth from the orbit of a spacecraft was severely limited by the small number of photographs that had been made available to the public through the print media, together with too few sessions combining geography, geology, and photography in our Canadian Astronaut Program.

Although it will be a challenge to perform the science experiments successfully in a weightless environment where everything floats, for me the best thing about the voyage will be the unique opportunity to view the Earth from space. Throughout the years, astronauts have captured the light of our world and of worlds beyond through photography. Each frame is not only a historical record of the planet's features that can be catalogued, reviewed, and compared flight to flight, it is also a record of human endeavour. The fact that a human being is "up there" is evidenced by the return to Earth of film from many different camera types, all loaded by humans, and exposed by humans. The Earth is literally seen through the eyes of an astronaut. Before manned space flight, this was not possible.

Back in 1962, astronaut John Glenn began to record the awesome beauty of our planet from the *Mercury Friendship 7* capsule. Since that time, upwards of one hundred thousand photographs of the Earth from space have been entered into the NASA Earth Observation Databank. Recording the history of our planet by means of space photography is not a simple matter of packing a road map and a point-and-shoot camera after reading the instruction book on how to change the film. Good photographic results from Earth-viewing depend on three factors: a receptive, committed crew member; correct training, both in Earth observation and in Earth photography; and the equipment itself, which includes all the lenses, films, filters, spot meters, and any new, improved gadgetry flying on the mission.

All crew members who have time available away from the busy schedule of on-orbit activities are able to use any one of a wide assortment of cameras to capture the Earth at one moment in time. The training of crew members has changed significantly since the *Mercury* missions. Now astronauts take mandatory courses in flight-specific Earth observation and the use of cameras.

In the *Apollo* program, the focus was on observing the lunar landscape — in preparation for mankind's first steps on another planetary body — rather than on observing Earth. During the *Apollo 8* mission, for example, more than seven hundred photographs of the moon were taken compared to about one hundred fifty photographs of the planet. It was the first opportunity to study certain features of the lunar surface free from the atmospheric distortion that is inherent in telescopic photography from Earth.

By the time *Apollo 11* launched from Cape Kennedy on July 16, 1969, for its nine-day lunar landing mission, space photography had advanced even further. The prime photographic objective of *Apollo 11* was to photograph the lunar surface — specifically "targets of opportunity," or scientifically interesting sites, and potential *Apollo* landing sites. Mission planners also wanted photographs of various lunar activities after landing, including man's first step onto the surface of the moon. There was a limited quantity of photographic equipment that could be floated to the moon, however, and as a result, the photographic requirements could be achieved only through creative selection and preparation of both cameras and film. For instance, above-atmosphere photography must include consideration of fogging or premature exposure of film, because radiation in space is greater than it is on the Earth. *Apollo 11* returned with 1,359 frames of 70-mm photography, 17 pairs of lunar-surface stereoscopic photographs, and 58,134 frames of 16-mm photography.

Later *Apollo* missions incorporated recommendations made by earlier crew and ground support personnel to improve the quality of the pictures. *Apollo 17*, in particular, achieved a significant advance in Earth observation. For the first time, the Antarctic continent was captured in a full view of the globe. It probably would not have been too difficult to exhaust the on-board film supplies photographing the beautiful, vibrant colours reflected from structures such as the Great Barrier Reef in preference to the main target of opportunity, the black-and-white surface of the moon.

Earth observation and Earth photography were boosted aloft in the United States' first manned space station, *Skylab*. Compared to today's shuttle flights at an average altitude of 300 km (162 naut. mi.), its orbit was at a moderate-to-high altitude of 435 km (235 naut. mi.) above the equator, with its path varying between 50 degrees north and 50 degrees south. From the launch of the first *Skylab* crew on May 25, 1973, to the return of the third and final crew on February 8, 1974, a total of 35,704 frames of Earth photographs were acquired. In this time, *Skylab* orbited every ninety-three minutes, covering the band between 50 degrees north and 50 degrees south of the equator every five days. Although weather and crew-member schedules precluded continuous operation of the photographic equipment during daylight periods, *Skylab* provided a giant leap forward in the ability of human beings to capture images of the planet.

After a seven-year hiatus, the United States returned to space on April 12, 1981, on board the orbiter *Columbia* at an altitude of 268 km (145 naut. mi.) for thirty-six orbits at 40 degrees above and below the equator. This historic flight of the Space Transportation System (STS) and the next three shuttle flights acquired more than twenty-two hundred photographs of the Earth with 70-mm cameras. For these initial missions, preflight lectures to the crew were given by an *ad hoc* scientific investigative team. Today NASA's unique Space Shuttle Earth Observations Project (SSEOP) combines the two powerful fields of Earth observation and Earth photography from space. It provides coordinated crew training in the Earth sciences preflight, support during the missions, and cataloguing and distribution of the photographs and information postflight.

My preflight training, as for all astronauts aboard the space shuttle, included sessions with professional photographers at NASA as well as scientists in the Earth Observation Office. The academic backgrounds of these scientists include geology, geography, computer science, and environmental studies, to name a few. Each crew member is provided with a preflight training manual with extensive colour reproductions and captions as well as cartographic information on specific places to photograph on that particular mission. These targets of opportunity vary according to the altitude of the orbiter, the inclination or latitude flown above and below the equator, the season in which the mission is being flown, and specific scientific interests such as natural phenomena (volcanoes, for example) and man-made phenomena (burning oil wells). Particular areas that are photographed on each shuttle flight are also indicated in the manual.

The value of documenting the evolution of the Earth is emphasized to each astronaut team that flies. This requires many sessions on types of landforms, vegetation patterns, and dynamic features that occur on the outer crust of the planet. Although most shuttle flights are of fairly short duration compared to the *Skylab* program, weather patterns that preclude photographing certain areas of interest may dissipate towards the end of the mission, allowing completion of an Earth-observation photographic objective. I have to be ready for whatever opportunity presents itself.

Before the flight, the Earth-observation personnel presented a summary of the desired Earth sites and recommended techniques for obtaining the best possible pictures. This is not to rule out creative photography on the part of the astronauts, but rather to provide guidance that will prove very helpful in the weightless environment of space, where just restraining ourselves to be able to photograph will entail a major expense in energy and concentration.

We're going to do it! I wonder briefly whether I'll have to use any of my bail-out training. Even in this modest amount of light, the bail-out cue card is visible, stuck on a mid-deck locker. It is awe-inspiring to be sitting here, looking at a checklist in this green glow. Just beyond my big black boots that will protect my feet if things get out of hand, the cue card details two bail-out sequences. The only thing left to think about now is keeping the differences in the two scenarios, or modes, clear in my mind. In the first one — that's *before* the liftoff — I need to take *off* the chute before rolling out of the chair. If I have to use the "Mode 1 pad egress" to get out in an emergency situation on the launch pad, it will be unassisted and will take place in the next three minutes. One more time through the checklist:

Visor down and locked.

Pull the green apple.

Pull the quick-disconnect/lap belts.

Release chute.

Evacuate.

Slide wire.

In the second bail-out sequence, *after* the launch, I keep the parachute *on*. It's so automatic now. One glance at the cue card, and I'll plug into the right escape mode.

The launch of Discovery on January 22, 1992.

As we leave the Earth, I sing to myself:

O Canada,
Our home and native land!
True patriot love . . .

F L O A T I N G   I N   S P A C E

JANUARY 22, 1992

DISCOVERY/HOUSTON: WE SEE A NOMINAL MECO. NO OMS-1 REQUIRED AND YOU'RE A GO FOR THE ET PHOTO DTO.

ROGER. NOMINAL MECO. NO OMS-1. GO FOR ET PHOTO DTO.

SUDDENLY THERE IS NO MORE acceleration and no more pressure on my body. It is like being at the top of a roller coaster and my whole body is in free-fall. My helmet is no longer heavy. Everything feels like it wants to float away from me, even the camera that I am assisting with, which will record the external tank as it falls from the shuttle towards the Earth's atmosphere. After the photos are taken and our final orbit correction is completed, I will unstrap myself from my seat in the mid-deck and remove my launch/entry suit.

An astronaut is thought not to have them, not during the ride to Launch Complex 39A, or during the thundering liftoff. But as I float up towards the flight deck, the butterflies are definitely there. It is a wonderful sensation going up the ladder from the mid-deck without having to place one foot above the other, and I revel in living in an age that surpasses anything found in the fantasies of Jules Verne or the adventures of Flash Gordon. A lifetime of coping with issues of role and gender vanish as I am transported back to the innocence, energy, and imagination of my youth. These childhood qualities never really left me, but I certainly have been bruised by struggling upstream on Earth, following my dream against all odds. Now I am floating without oppressive words and deeds to impede my way. The only thing that brushes by me is the edge of the "attic" — the communal mid-deck roof and flight-deck floor.

As I lift my head to see light streaming in from the flight-deck windows, I feel more than the usual stomach awareness of space flight. I have anticipated this precious moment since the 1950s when I played with plastic model planes, rockets, satellites, and a space station; worked on a school project about the moon; and pored over the worn covers and pages of my science-fiction books or my favourite *National Geographic* magazines. It is important to capture it all, and to bring back as much of it as I can to share with my space pal from long ago, my sister Barbara. My mom will be waiting eagerly for details of this exciting adventure, too. She and my dad always supported our exploits with enthusiasm. Dad, however, didn't have to withstand the emotions of the launch. I have missed him a great deal since his death two months before the *Challenger* accident on January 28, 1986.

Flashing through my mind is the wish that I could again flip back in time, if only for a few seconds, to show that little girl from McGregor Avenue that she was going to do it! I am beaming as I float up into the nest of tethered cameras, lazily drifting in the air currents. My world, my planet Earth, is waiting just beyond my line of sight. With an exhilarating final course correction, I push off the flight-deck floor and head towards the windows in the aft flight deck. The lump in my throat gives way to a murmur then a stifled cry. There it is. All the View-Master reels and all the shuttle photographs did not prepare me for this emotional rendezvous with the planet that I had lived upon, studied, and thought I knew.

Is there any successful way to prepare yourself for an emotional event? Probably not. Performing a science experiment, or taking a picture, is a trainable activity, but no one can prepare you for the overwhelming experience of being in visual contact with Earth from space. Many people have asked me what it is like to float in orbit, watching the world go by, and all I can tell them is that it is an awesome adventure.

My impression is that each crew member lives and relives Earth-viewing in an extremely personal manner, some challenged spiritually or intellectually more than others by the contrast between the black universe and the bright pastel Earth. Many questions arise when you are removed from your preflight, Earthbound mind-set and faced with the reality that there is nothing else around you but black, inhospitable space. Some astronauts believe more firmly in previously held convictions; others find strength in a new perspective that makes the activities of mankind seem curiously distant and diminutive. I personally feel the need to balance both space and terrestrial perspectives to achieve an all-encompassing view of mankind's position in space and time as a life-form on planet Earth.

The first moon missions transformed our Earth-centred thinking by giving us a view of the globe from the perspective of "out there" — the realm beyond the Earth's crust and atmosphere. When I see those glorious photographs taken by the astronauts on the *Apollo* missions, I feel a curious sense of relief that there is now proof of what was once only scientific theory — that our Earth is round. We cannot duplicate those lunar views of Earth last photographed in 1972, because both the shuttle and Russia's MIR space station circle our planet in low Earth orbit — too close to see Earth as more than a segment of a sphere. The lunar vision of Earth, however, as a blue and white marble suspended in the black universe, is preserved on stickers, cards, backpacks, sweatshirts, and logos.

Seen from inside the flight deck of the orbiter, the planet is framed by man-made objects. The windows encase landscapes that sweep by beyond my reach. The layers of glass that preserve life on the shuttle also prevent close contact with the light of the distant glowing treasure, which someone named "Earth." When I was young and eager for adventure, I was inspired by the images of light in the illustrations in the Classic Comics' versions of *From Earth to the Moon* and *King Solomon's Mines* — images of solar eclipses and glittering treasures inside great wooden chests. Even now I associate light with certain images, emotions, and feelings.

Viewed from space, the Earth, like the moon, reflects the sun. Unlike the moon, however, Earth emits its own energy and light in the forms of fire, lightning, volcanic eruptions, and auroras. During space flight, when the light angles are favourable between the sun and the Earth, and between the orbiter and the reflected sunlight from the Earth, I am absorbed by the planet and the soft strength of its shimmering blue atmosphere. With my headset off and no one else floating by in the flight deck, there are no distractions from this visual surround. Photographs will never replace this real-time experience. As vivid as images from the film industry, holograms, and virtual reality can be, none will ever have the emotional impact of actual reality, the urgency of "now."

In space, the atmosphere is three-dimensional, whereas on Earth, I view it as the sky that begins at the horizon, a two-dimensional object. On the ground, the atmosphere is all around us, but we can see it only along the horizon and above us as sky. In space, there is no "above," unless you think of your head as "up" and everything beyond your head as "above." In space, a sunset or a sunrise may appear in the same view as the night sky, and the atmosphere, which looks like a rainbow, appears in three dimensions.

When I stand on the surface of the Earth, the horizon seems to last forever, because the planet is curved: as I walk, something will always appear ahead of me. The horizon remains stationary, framed by a sunset or the blue sky. The Earth appears infinitely large. In space, this curved line of the horizon is also continuous, but I can see the surface features of a sphere. The horizon is finite, so I see a finite Earth.

Beyond Earth, on the other hand, there is seemingly infinite space.

As I look down, across, and above from the flight-deck window, the shining planet curves from left to right. I have never in my life seen anything as big as this. The sheet of oceans and land masses moves like a rolling ball edged in black, but from this altitude I can never see the whole of the ball at one time. The immense arc moves as if it were running on the spot. Although the shapes of certain structures on this slice of Earth are familiar, they have never been assembled in my mind in this orientation.

The other windows reveal the separation of planet and universe. The edge of the arc, Earth's "limb" as it is called, protects the planet from the absence of colour, the blackness of the universe that surrounds me. This black is very black, if one can talk of degrees of black. The best description I can offer is to call it *profoundly* black. Unless there is something out there near the horizon to reflect the sun's light back to my eyes, like the passing moon, or a planet such as Venus, there is nothing to draw my eyes away from the full light of the glowing Earth. I feel bathed in its coloured light — reds, browns, greens, whites, blues. And the most beautiful of all these colours, the one that I associate with the many emotions I feel? Overwhelmingly, it is blue. Blues that curve around and engulf the limb. Blues that appear to be a form of living fibre-optic light, yet soft and iridescent. If it were not for the glass window, my hand might stretch out and touch this thin canopy under which our spinning planet glides so quietly and peacefully. The atmosphere dominates my first view of the Earth from space and remains in my memory as an experience of colour and emotion intertwined.

So many times during space flight, I reflect back to my high school geography and history classes, and the training with the Earth observation experts in Canada and at the Johnson Space Center in Houston, Texas. If I were SPOC (the Shuttle Programmable Onboard Computer), I would know every territory that drifts by. But then, if I were a computer, how could I feel? How could I smile from within as I play amongst the clouds and follow the curve of a coastline from so far away? In exploring the borderless land and water masses from the windows of the spacecraft, I can sense the history and varied cultures of the Earth unfolding before my eyes. As an explorer on the ground, or even in an airplane, I would be too close.

On the planet, we are so small that we can be confused about a boundary. Oceans seem forbidding, and mountain ranges divide one part of a country from another. My view on the surface of Earth ends at the horizon. On a clear day, from the top of a mountain or mesa in the southwestern United States, the horizon spreads out over 160 km (100 mi.) in one direction. In space, from the shuttle's average altitude of 300 km (162 naut. mi.), I can see about 2000 km (1,200 mi.) in one direction. The oceans are connections rather than boundaries. All land and water masses fit exactly together. As I traverse the Earth at a speed of 8 km (5 mi.) per second, in one minute I may pass over countries with lakes and rivers too numerous to count and, just a few minutes later, bake in the same sunlight that is scorching sand dunes in a desert below.

From a high altitude I have an encompassing view and can see in all directions. However, although the distances appear small, the resolution of the human eye is only powerful enough to recognize large blocks of land and sea. In other words, from the shuttle, I don't look at the planet in pieces but as a whole object, because that is what greets my eye during each ninety-minute orbit. For example, from the altitude of low Earth orbit, I can appreciate the relationship of the Himalayas to China and Tibet on one side, and to Nepal and the sloping plains of India sweeping into the ocean on the other. On the surface of the planet, these large features tend to fragment the Earth, and sometimes this feeling of fragmentation extends beyond the geophysical to such things as family and country — things that are supposed to bind us together through emotion and history. Up here I can fly over any country without permission, without having to worry about passports, politics, or air-traffic control.

In general, the land looks flat; there is no way to separate hills from plains, or swamps from wooded areas. But I can distinguish features in the desert, such as the fascinating array of ridges, mounds, and even sandstars. It is over the desert, too, that the land explodes into broad expanses of boldly marked colours. The big sand seas contrast sharply with the harder surface along which the dunes creep. This shifting of sand is not seen from space, because the shuttle is travelling too fast and too high.

In space, there is no weather. "Weather" occurs in the atmosphere closer to Earth. On any given day when there is sunshine on Earth, I

Whereas
crescent dunes
are formed by
prevailing
winds, these
star dunes in
the Sahara are
formed by
variable
winds, which
have blown
the sand into
several "arms"
radiating
from a central
point.

The delicate
white pinwheel
of a tropical
cyclone.

can go outside, lie on my back, look up, and soak in the different colours and patterns of cloud, blue sky, and flying creatures. But the broader horizon in space gives me the unique perspective of being on top of clouds looking out over vast distances. It creates a visual and emotional image that is much different than any I have experienced on Earth. A storm that I know is wreaking havoc on the planet becomes a source of beauty and inspiration. Water vapour in a hurricane, for instance, becomes a delicate white pinwheel. It fills me with curiosity and disbelief. Here I am floating above it, drinking hot chocolate and listening to music during my lunch break or in my pre-sleep period, while below that level of cloud, there is life trying to cope with the inevitable natural forces that shape the planet.

From my perspective high above, I can place my hand against the window and cover a whole storm front. I feel as if I could fly down, untouched by the violent wind and rain that I can neither see, feel, nor hear, and clutch mankind and other life to me and return to the relative safety of space. But I can't. Only my imagination can. Space will never be a permanent refuge from these powerful Earth forces, although science in the future may be able to find better ways to cope with them on the surface.

To see the Earth from space is, in my view, like meeting someone whom I have read about and admired for many years. When we do meet special people in our lives, we may wish later that we had had a camera to capture and preserve the encounter, although on reflection we may realize that taking a picture at such a time would have been intrusive and would have ruined rather than preserved the moment. In space flight, on the other hand, I have it all — cameras, professional training in their use, and an extraordinary subject, the Earth. Each second from space grants me a new wonder and a new chance to capture forever on film the endearing landscape below, which looks like a painting or tapestry.

A free-floating observer and photographer of planetary phenomena faces significant challenges, however. As much as space travellers are considered to be superpeople, the ability to see objects at a great distance depends on many logistical and physical factors, in addition to the amount of training and the receptiveness of the observer. For instance, up to one-third of all space travellers have reported some change in either their reading- or distance-vision. One theory is that shifting fluids within the eye itself may alter the evenness of the retina or produce a change in the contour of the cornea. I was lucky. I wore my glasses during the launch but didn't need them again until I returned to Earth. Wearing them in space made me feel sick and without them I could see the Himalayas crisply out the porthole in the Spacelab.

The reduced gravity of space flight provides another challenge to photographers. It's a truism that everything floats in space. But not just bodies and camera equipment take on a life of their own; absolutely anything and everything floats, including crumbs of food and even body oils. Cleaning the windows of the orbiter is an exercise in patience. As soon as the window is clean, something drifts by and sticks onto the pristine surface between the camera lens and the Earth. Luckily, unless it's a large object, it won't block too much light or appear as a blurry image on the film.

Because the orbiter is travelling so quickly, it is essential to be wedged in place and ready to shoot before a "target of opportunity" appears. Floating cameras are one thing, but my free-floating body will add even more movement to the film. And there's always the danger that the edge of the window, a body part, or a piece of debris floating around in the flight deck will obscure the view.

Once these problems are solved, I have to be ready to detect that something is there for me to see as I pass over any given site. Obviously, it helps to recognize what your photographic subject is! A preflight training manual, *The Astronaut's Guide to Terrestrial Impact Craters*, has been developed to help us identify certain land structures. In flight, we have an atlas with minimal lines and borders, identifying only places that can be seen from the low Earth orbit in which the shuttle flies. And there is SPOC, which tells us in real time where the orbiter is, using a schematic diagram of the orbit path over the Earth. It also provides information on Earth night and day patterns as well as camera settings for photographing a specific site.

Once the window is clean, the camera is loaded, and I am wedged in place, I hope that the sun has not set, which it does every ninety minutes. The low light levels just before Earth's twilight provide a wonderfully rich colour, but film to date is not adequate, even with the aid of current lenses, to capture many of the features in the fading light below.

Although the Earth rotates beyond me as I skim above it, there is no sense of motion on the surface itself. No movement of waves or wind. My sense of motion outside the shuttle is confined to the frequent display of sunrises and sunsets, moonrises and moonsets. In fact, the only movement I see that originates from the planet is caused by the effects of light in the atmosphere rather than on the Earth's surface.

There are several layers to our atmosphere. The tropopause extends from ground level up to 16 km (10 mi.) and holds all our weather phenomena. The stratosphere extends 16 to 48 km (10 to 30 mi.), and the mesosphere from 48 to 80 km (30 to 50 mi.). Between 80 and 480 km (50 and 298 mi.), in what is called the thermosphere, the temperature changes rapidly. It is within this layer that the shuttle flies and the aurora are visible.

For those who have not experienced either the aurora borealis in the Northern Hemisphere or the aurora australis in the Southern Hemisphere, it is hard to imagine the way this light expands outward from the atmosphere into space. It is an incredible sight. The shimmering fingers and curtains of light are the result of the solar wind — an excitation of the Earth's atmosphere near the poles by radiation from the sun. As the solar wind courses through the geomagnetic field and upper atmosphere, electrical energy is generated, driving ionized particles into denser gases below. This produces a light show without sound, which with its lines, loops, closed circles, patches, and vertical pencils of light can use up many magazines of film. Most auroras emanate a greenish-white glow, the colour given off by ionized oxygen. In the Northern Hemisphere in the heart of winter, observers on the ground may see a vertical curtain varying in length and intensity, like a supernatural pipe organ. Or they may see streams of fluorescent-green light particles that drift in the night sky in swirls and flowing lines like sand washed ashore at the edge of an ocean. We have never created fireworks the equal of an aurora.

Lightning is another natural phenomenon that is visible from space and that provides Earth observers with a sense of movement. From space, lightning is a soft, nonthreatening glimpse of something dynamic, something alive on the planet. Although it appears in various forms close to the surface — as "sheet lightning" or "fork lightning," for example — in space flight we don't see defined lightning forks. Eruptions of light from a large storm front are visible to the astronaut for a few minutes while lightning tries to escape from under a cloud layer. It is reminiscent of Christmas lights that are strung on trees then covered with a thick blanket of snow. The diffusion of the light

through the snow is similar to the muffled burst of energy which can be seen from space.

Astronauts occasionally see phenomena that are totally celestial, although I didn't see any on our flight. Meteors acquire light as they penetrate the Earth's dense atmosphere and are set aglow by the heat generated when a rock meets a hard place. They are actually debris from comets or asteroids. The long streak that can be seen from Earth is the accumulation of heated particles that remain visible as long as they are hot enough. Meteors usually burn up before reaching the ground, although a few particles do manage to touch down sometimes. With five to ten meteors striking the Earth's atmosphere per hour, it is fortunate that few of them are large enough to penetrate the tropopause.

We don't often see man-made events from space, but when we do it's not always a positive experience. During the Persian Gulf War in 1991, astronauts reported seeing tiny, bright points of light that were actually huge oil well fires. On the other hand, the delicate light patterns of large cities lying beyond the windows of the spacecraft are cosy reminders of loved ones and fellow Earth dwellers. At night there is no distinction between land and sea except for these lacy displays of light, which are not the brilliant neon colours that we see on the ground but a yellowish-white monotone. The intricate network of lights in the populous industrialized areas of North America, Europe, and Japan contrasts with the more extensive areas of the world that, with little or no power, are bathed in darkness.

By day, we cross over many areas that appear unfamiliar to me at first. This usually occurs when I'm not looking at SPOC or the atlas. The orbiter flies in unusual patterns: sometimes the windows face south, so the Earth appears to be upside down. Even when my eye does focus on a geographical site, we pass over it so quickly that there is little time to absorb what I am seeing.

Many tourists like to travel without cameras so that they are not distracted from the experience or the insights of the moment. Understandably, they do not want to have their eyes buried behind a viewfinder for fear of missing the forest for the trees. The only drawback, of course, is the inability to retain the vision or emotion for accurate recall days, weeks, months, or years later. Nowhere is this truer than in space flight. The Grand Canyon is extraordinary, but how can I re-create the leafy pattern of the canyon in words that are as precise and emotion-filled as a photograph?

With the light beam of the sun gliding over the surface of the Earth, water bodies beyond the windows reflect the sunlight back to my eyes, revealing small lakes. The identification of various land and water features often depends, though, upon associated geological features. For example, it is much easier to distinguish the river Nile and the irrigated strip of land beside it because of the contrasting desert that surrounds it than it is to see large rivers that are encased by foliage and dark-coloured rocks in the Cambrian Shield. Seasonal changes help to identify these areas that appear to be monochromatic. In the summer, shorelines are distinctive because water and land are easily separated. The road patterns or airports of an urban area, however, barely appear in a photograph taken on a summer flight. During winter flights like mine, a little dusting of snow helps distinguish these features from the surrounding landscape.

Man-made structures are difficult to recognize with the naked eye. The Great Wall of China has reportedly been seen by other astronauts, but there is no photograph of it registered on film in the giant SSEOP film catalogue. I cherish the times when I see something that is

The rim of the Grand Canyon, which perches 1200 to 1370 m (4,000 to 4,500 ft.) above the Colorado River in Arizona, looks like a piece of a leaf from the shuttle.

Like the Grand Canyon, Canyon de Chelly in Arizona is a steep-sided canyon that was formed by the erosive force of water cutting through soft rock.

evidence of our civilization on Earth and am especially excited when I identify my hometown of Sault Ste. Marie, Ontario. Most large cities are clearly visible, and it is usually easy to appreciate the physiographic features that help explain why a city was located in a certain area, such as access to a water supply or strategic importance. The bigger the city, the less I need to rely on a very high-powered telephoto lens to provide me with a definite siting or identification. Industrialized cities are more easily distinguished, not only by their generally larger sizes, the denudation of the surrounding land, and the larger number of lights at night, but also by the differences in materials used for constructing buildings. During the day, non-industrialized cities tend to blend into the surrounding landscape because their buildings are constructed of mud, clay bricks, or other locally available materials.

Although I cherish looking out the windows to see Earth, I am preoccupied with the real reason why I am in space. The main set of science experiments, or "payload," is carried out in the Spacelab, located in the back of the Payload Bay and connected by tunnel to the mid-deck in the front of the shuttle. The experiments occupy my every moment that isn't taken up with the activities of daily living such as sleeping, eating, and changing my clothes. This flight was originally scheduled to be a ten-day mission. The change in orbiters, from *Columbia* to *Atlantis* and then to *Discovery*, meant that it was

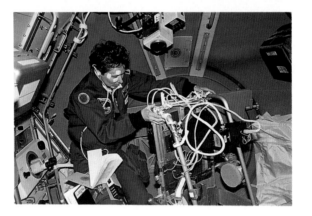

The microgravity vestibular investigations (MVI) chair was used to observe the effects of weightlessness on the balance system of the body. My eye movements were recorded as I was spun in the chair. In this photograph, I am checking the connections between the chair and the control box .

impossible for NASA to put all the experiments into a relaxed timeline, or schedule, for the crew. Because *Discovery* can't keep the heavy Spacelab aloft for as long as the more powerful *Columbia* can, the ten days have been compressed into seven.

To avoid compromising the science experiments, various measures have been taken, such as involving the three orbiter crew members — the commander, the pilot, and the flight engineer — whose job descriptions normally do not include science detail as a primary task.

Before the change in orbiters, the four payload crew members, whose main task is to conduct the science experiments, had more time scheduled in the first few days of orbit to take into account the inefficiency of performing experiments in space, equipment malfunction, and our own physiological adjustments to weightlessness. That is history. The reality is that this flight has ended up as a seven-day mission, which has now been extended since the launch to eight days. The extra time would have been very welcome earlier in the flight, when the twelve-hour payload shift turned into sixteen or more hours in order to complete activities on the same mission day as planned.

I spend many hours working at Biorack, a small biology lab developed by the European Space Agency, which also built Spacelab. It contains a glovebox, which is a closed environmental system where we can perform experiments without fear of toxic chemicals or soil particles escaping and getting into our eyes or out into the shuttle. The box is accessed by long rubber gloves. Even when I am working at Biorack, however, I can float away to the aft porthole, the only window in Spacelab, to catch glimpses of Canada as we sail by. The orbiter crew always give me a shout on the intercom when we're coming up on an area that they know is of special interest to me. If the experimental procedure that I am working on is in a holding pattern, I can easily float back to the window without harming the experiment.

The view from Spacelab is incredible. Its window is closer to the Earth than any other shuttle window, with the orbiter tail facing the planet. Unfortunately, all the 70-mm cameras are located up on the flight deck, leaving me with only a 35-mm camera, which I know will not capture Earth as clearly. I'll have to let my eyes and brain capture the colours below.

The rich blues of the ocean, the exquisite turquoise of the Great Barrier Reef, and the soft white snows of winter are soothing to eyes that have been engrossed in demanding scientific duties. Greens and browns predominate on the landscape except when we fly over deserts. These provide the greatest visual contrast — green vegetation against beige sand, dried salt pans against iron-laden red sand. The wide range of individual shades that I have come to expect from walking through a greenhouse, or even looking in my mid-deck locker for a brightly coloured polo shirt (the upper-body apparel of the shuttle astronaut), are absent.

In space flight, the only sounds I hear are scientific exchanges, instrument noise, crew member chatter, and music from tapes selected pre-launch for off-duty enjoyment. Before my mission, I carefully chose music and sounds that would remind me of my youthful dream of becoming a space explorer. "One Moment in Time" and the theme song from the film *Return of the Jedi* fill my pre-sleep hours. For Earth viewing, I picked out a selection of emotional melodies — "Nothing like the Freedom" and "From a Distance" — and for special interest passes, "Oh Canada" and "The Star Spangled Banner" — musical renditions played by my aunt on the organ and piano, and vocal renditions performed in a deep, stirring voice by a policeman from my hometown. If that doesn't test tear-duct secretions in weightlessness, I can play pre-taped messages from my family and friends, music from a variety of Canadian artists and a high school band, and Girl Guide songs.

It is very easy to become so involved in the technical and scientific aspects of this Spacelab flight that I overlook something that I love most about living on our planet: the sounds of the Earth itself. Looking at the blue-and-white world that fills my heart, I cannot hear what is beyond the windows. The Earth is silent. I cannot hear the plaintive cry of a Swainson's thrush, the piercing echoes of a blue jay, or even the conversational barking of a dog. In fact, the planet seems devoid of anything that might be able to communicate with me.

From the perspective of space, the many generations of life-forms that have existed on the planet are nowhere to be found. I wonder, from time to time, what Earth might have looked like during the emergence of humans as a species, or even what secrets could have been gleaned from such a distance about the fate of the dinosaurs. Like the dinosaurs, our species may also be temporary and transient. From space, it is difficult to ignore that I am merely a life-form, and like all other life-forms on Earth, I depend on this wonderful planet for survival. Without it and its resources, I would cease to exist.

This conviction is deepened by looking out into the blackness of the universe, where the only relief comes from light reflected from a far-off planet, such as Venus, or from the moon. There are distant pinpricks of light upon which the shuttle relies for celestial alignment and navigation. These stars remain distant wonders, which, because they no longer shimmer, have lost their terrestrial living nature. A cold foreboding sweeps over me, looking away from the Earth. There is nothing else that can support life as I know it. It is little wonder that I quickly look back at the Earth for reassurance that I do have a home.

I now perceive home and myself, though, in a different way. On the ground, visual imagery bombards me daily, assuring me that I am the superior life-form on Earth. But I wonder. The great distance above the ground in which I am floating changes my Earthbound mind-set. The Rockies become rows of crisply defined mounds, and the Himalayas, a chaotic collection of small stalagmites. In one pass, it is difficult to pinpoint the great one, Mount Everest, in the vast sea of other ice-covered peaks. On Earth, we climb these mountains to answer an inner challenge, "because it's there." "Conquering" Everest demonstrates our courage and our ability to persevere against all odds. Such feats become high-profile events when they haven't been done before, if they require great physical or mental stamina, or if they set us "against" a naturally occurring phenomena. Interesting, the Earth perception. From out here, I don't attach the same importance to what now appears to be a remote event on a tiny part of the Earth's crust. In space, I feel like a pretty

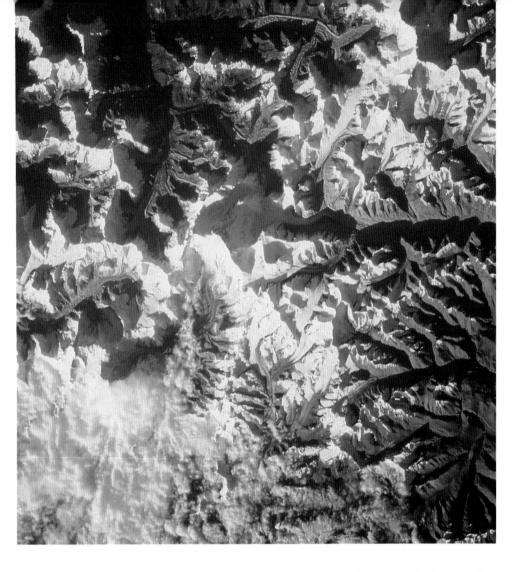

Mount Everest, the highest mountain in the world, sits on the border between Nepal and China, almost at the centre of this photograph.

small, fragile life-form. The huge physical presence that I see below will endure long after I and my kind are gone.

From space, the beauty of the outer crust and the atmosphere grasps the most emotional part of my soul. The effects of the many forces of nature that have shaped and reshaped this planet over time become very clear in space flight. Studying the past is one way to understand the Earth, and space flight can contribute enormously to our knowledge of the evolution of the planet. If I could have been here 100 million years ago, at a distance safe enough to view the Earth, and taken freeze-frame pictures every 100 years or so, how much better I would understand who we are today! The photographs that we take now are those freeze-frames that future generations will use to understand their place in time.

The age of the Earth, estimated by uranium dating, is currently thought to be 4.6 billion years. Until approximately 3.9 billion years ago, when the first life-forms appeared, the Earth was bombarded by meteors, asteroids, and comets. The effects of these impacts were far-reaching and have been credited with the development of ocean basins and continents.

Of all the heavenly bodies that crashed into Earth throughout the millennia, only about one hundred impact craters have been identified to date on the surface of the planet. In the Canadian Shield, there are many craters that are up to 450 million years old. We can see them from space in this area more easily than in other areas because of the slow geological changes in the surrounding land. Many craters are destroyed relatively quickly as a result of erosion and filling in by wind-borne soil and plant growth. Evidence of their existence is found in fragments recovered at suspected sites and in nearby rocks and minerals that formed because of the immense heat and pressures caused on impact. No matter how long ago these impacts occurred, new information still surfaces. For example, a crater covered by 65 million years of sediment, and possibly made by a celestial object some 16 km (10 mi.) across, was found in 1990 off the coast of the Yucatan peninsula in Mexico. The crater measures 297 km (185 mi.) in diameter. Research continues in order to discover whether or not the object divided into two fragments on striking the Earth's atmosphere, with the second fragment crashing into the Pacific. It is just as well I was not flying in a spacecraft observing primeval Earth when this incident occurred, although it would have been fascinating to watch — from a safe distance.

It is interesting to compare one of these meteors to the orbiter in terms of size and speed. A meteor that is at least 30 m (98 ft.) across or larger can enter the atmosphere at an average speed of 25 km (16 mi.) per second. The orbiter part of the shuttle has a length of 37.24 m (122.17 ft.) and flies around the Earth at an average speed of 8 km (5 mi.) per second. So it is much slower and much smaller than a meteor. To return to Earth, the orbiter decelerates in a controlled manner, using the belly of the craft, which is sheathed in black ceramic tiles to absorb the heat created by the friction of striking the dense atmosphere. To date, there is nothing man-made that is as large and fast as a big meteor and that can traverse the Earth's atmosphere without being reduced in size and certainly in speed.

Impact crater sites are photographed from space using different

The Manicouagan impact crater in Quebec is outlined by the waters of the Manicouagan Reservoir. The structure's ring-like halo and radiating fracture lines are more visible from space in the winter (inset) than in the summer (right).

camera positions — either above or to the side of the structure. Subtle features are more visible at sunset or sunrise, when the sun sits very low on the horizon, making shadows very long. Lake Manicouagan, an impact crater in Quebec, was photographed from space as early as the *Skylab* missions. It is quite striking and serves as a definite geological marker for the northeast portion of North America. Although the crater itself is 100 km (62 mi.) in diameter, it has a "halo" that extends outward to about 150 km (93 mi.) from the centre. It is easier to spot now than it would have been earlier this century, because today it is the site of a reservoir which is clearly outlined in the winter by snow and ice.

Each shuttle mission carries with it the exciting prospect of discovering one or more craters in the southern continents of Africa, Australia, and South America. Lighting conditions and seasonal changes, however, may hinder spotting an impact crater, even with the best intent and effort. Unfortunately, the heavy workload on-board this Spacelab flight precludes viewing all of the areas covered by *Discovery*. It is unlikely that any of the crew will spot a new crater this time.

On other flights, astronauts have seen evidence of the hot centre of the Earth in the form of eruption clouds spewing from volcanoes. Shuttle crew members were able to record pre- and post-eruption photographic overviews of Mount Pinatubo, which erupted in the Philippines in June 1991. This unexpected and violent eruption was the largest of this century, with more than 14 trillion kg (30 trillion lb.) of rock, dust, liquid, and gas exploding into the air, drifting over the surrounding countryside, and rising up into the atmosphere. The effects of the Mount Pinatubo eruption have been recorded worldwide, in both the dust in sunsets photographed from space and in the temperature change of Earth's fragile biosphere. Oxygen and water vapour normally present in the stratosphere combined with sulphur dioxide gas from the eruption to produce sulphuric acid droplets. These droplets bounce sunlight back into space, which has the effect of cooling the planet.

Although more volcanoes that are active have been identified in recent years, it is unlikely that volcanic activity on the Earth has increased. No doubt we have just improved our ability to identify such terrestrial events. After two hundred years of silence, the volcano at Krakatoa in Indonesia began erupting in May 1883, but it wasn't until August of that year that almost continuous explosive activity proved fatal for more than thirty-six thousand people living in the coastal villages. The sound of the explosion could be heard over 3000 km (1,860 mi.) away. In the hundred years that have followed this enormous disaster, advancements in science have enabled us to better understand the tremendous forces that constantly live below. Shuttle flights provide a unique vantage point from which to obtain critical overviews of areas of destruction and the regrowth of vegetation.

The ability of life-forms to exist on our constantly changing planet depends largely on climate, and our climate depends to a great extent on the moon. Even now, some think of the moon only as a night light, a tidal force, or a site for a good geological dig. What many people don't know is that the moon provides Earth with a stable wobble,

Inset: This photograph of Mount Pinatubo was taken ten years before its eruption in 1991. The volcano is visible in the upper right quarter of the picture.

Left: Mount Pinatubo, under cloud at the top of the photograph, erupted ten months before this photograph was taken. The rivers, which are grey with volcanic debris, were scarcely visible before the eruption.

Right: In this 1992 photograph of the rainbow-like atmosphere at sunrise, with the unlit Earth in the fore-ground and the darkness of space above, the greyish-red band below the white layer is composed of ash and sulphuric acid particles from the 1991 Mount Pinatubo eruption.

protecting us from extremes in climate fluctuations that would preclude life as we know it. Scientists believe that the size of the moon with respect to the Earth is perfect for human life to exist compared to the size of other moons and their planets in the solar system.

The moon, however, has not protected the Earth from ice ages and interglacial periods. The most recent ice age, which lasted one hundred thousand years, ended approximately ten thousand years ago. The Earth is like a top spinning, with a tilt, at moderate speeds around a central point. The spread and retreat of glacial ice is dependent upon the Earth's tilt and wobble. Twenty thousand years ago, the North American Ice Sheet covered all of Canada and the United States east of the Rockies. It receded to provide Greenland with an ice sheet 3000 m (9,800 ft.) thick and with large rivers of ice that flow towards the sea.

Recent evidence from an ice-core sample through 3 km (2 mi.) of ice in Greenland reveals that there have been dramatic changes in the Earth's climate in the past. The stable climate we have enjoyed during the lifetime of the human race may prove to be only a brief pause in a period of dynamic change. As a species, we may only exist during this period of time because of all the right factors being in the right place at the right time. You and I may be living in the only window of opportunity that may ever exist on planet Earth suitable for our survival here.

Many shuttle flights, unlike this one, do not fly near Greenland and other parts of the Earth that are covered in snow and ice, because of either the season in which the shuttle is launched, or the distance flown north or south of the equator. The contrast between Greenland's brightly reflecting white snow and the deep blue of the surrounding ocean is breathtaking (see page 6). It reminds me of the similar contrasting colours in the features of warmer climates — the white sands and turquoise waters of coral reefs, which are moments away in the shuttle. It hardly seems possible that a slight tilt of the planet or wobble in its orbit can mean the difference between a palm tree and an iceberg.

Scientists use photographs taken from space of glaciers to track their progression and to follow the ice masses that break off at their edges to become icebergs. Glaciers affect both physical and biological components of the living planet. They contain close to 90 percent of the world's fresh water and weigh an estimated 30.5 trillion t (30 trillion tons). It's impossible, though, to deal with the concept of weight in space, because I weigh nothing and the world also seems to weigh nothing. So when I look at the planet, even the icebergs breaking away from Greenland appear as tiny, floating specks.

Athough the continental crust cannot be described as being particularly spongy, the removal of the weight of the receding glaciers has allowed the land to rebound. Around Hudson Bay, half of the estimated 600 m (2,000 ft.) of land that lay beneath the glaciers for thousands of years has sprung back up. With an uplift of 60 cm (2 ft.) per century, Hudson Bay will be left high and dry when an equilibrium is reached in about five thousand years. From space, this rebounding land mass appears as parallel lines, which look like a giant's staircase. Farther to the south the Great Lakes, formed by the receding ice sheet, are filled with water from melted ice. They are

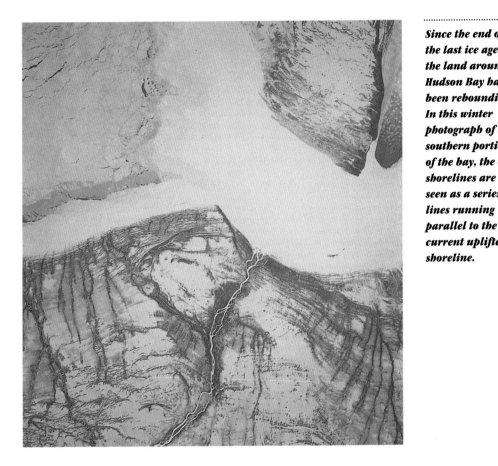

Since the end of the last ice age, the land around Hudson Bay has been rebounding. In this winter photograph of a southern portion of the bay, the old shorelines are seen as a series of lines running parallel to the current uplifted shoreline.

clearly visible from the shuttle as I fly over Canada and the northern United States.

In addition to glaciation, two other tremendous forces constantly sculpt the planet, their masterpieces transcending anything made by humans. Wind and water, either separately or combined, have shifted sand, carved rock, and etched the veins of river valleys worldwide. This living painting called Earth also encompasses the fourth dimension, that of time.

On Earth, we look upon sudden storms, such as cyclones, as tremendously drawn out events, when in reality they are just very brief flurries of artistic activity by the physical forces on our planet. Our sense of time is related to our own life span. It influences our relationships with other species on the planet as well as our attitudes towards physical events. Because we live longer than most other life-forms, we have an attitude of omnipotence; we feel that anything that doesn't live as long as us isn't as powerful as us, while anything that exists for a longer time is an oddity. Because we see ourselves as the "gold standard," it is difficult for us to acknowledge that the Earth has its own time frame that must be respected. When we change the landscape faster than the planet's natural forces would, the surrounding biological environment doesn't have the ability to compensate for our intrusions.

Deep in the heart of Australia, Uluru (the aboriginal word for "Great Pebble") rises up from the surrounding flat plain to a height of 360 m (1,180 ft.). Also called Ayers Rock, it is a rocky, reddish island in a sea of wind-eroded landscape. It is hard to believe that such a large Earth object is not visible from space. It has an almost extraterrestrial appearance and yet is a manifestation of ancient natural forces at work on Earth.

The weathering of the Earth's surface produces soil as well as sculpture through processes that are very slow from a technological point-of-view. Temperature changes, water movement, oxidation, frost, and crystal growth combine with the physical activities of plants and animals to break down the planet's surface. Even gravity is a persistent force, tugging at rock debris and creating mudflows, avalanches, and sinkholes.

Our lives as human beings depend on healthy soil. We can't eat soil, so we rely upon plants to convert it into a form through which we can acquire certain compounds needed for building body tissues. The development of agriculture has depended on rich deposits of soil, and as I work with plants in the Biorack glovebox, it is hard not to appreciate soil's great value.

Although Uluru, or Ayers Rock, in Australia is the world's largest monolith, it cannot be seen with the human eye from space.

We study plants in space for two reasons. The first reason is to find plants that will grow in a weightless environment so that a closed life-support system which recycles water, air, and soil can be developed for future explorations of space. On the ground, plants respond to gravity; if you plant a seed upside down in the garden, it will still grow right side up. In the Spacelab experiments, we are trying to differentiate between the various responses of plants to light and gravity. The second reason is a spinoff benefit from the first. The

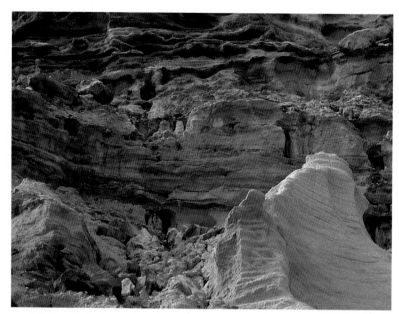

hybrid plants developed for space flight, in addition to coping with microgravity, will also have to cope with less than optimum water and soil conditions. These plant strains may eventually be more efficient users of the kinds of soils and limited resources we now have on Earth, particularly in developing countries.

From space, I assume that the different colours on the land masses are related to a variety of soils or land uses. The layering of soils and the variability in their organic content are suggested as I sweep my eyes over enormous stretches of changing colours in Africa. The desert sands are particularly noticeable. The largest desert on our planet, the Sahara, sprawls across an area approximately the size of the United States. The large sandseas, which cover over one-third of it, have

trapped sand for thousands of years in crescent dunes, ridges, and
star-shaped structures. From space, though, these red, yellow, orange,
and cream land-forms do not reveal their variety in height. Dunes may
rise from the surrounding surface from a third of a storey to over 120
storeys high, but I have little perception of this from the shuttle.

More than 55 million people live in the vast desert of the Sahara,
and 12 million of them rely on the resources of the desert itself, rather
than on either the Nile or the Niger rivers. The sensors of satellites can
trace the veins of old underground water systems, called "wadis," and
soon technology should be able to delineate large underground
storage systems of groundwater, called "aquifers." Had I launched six
thousand years ago, I would have seen a very different Sahara, one
not as arid as the Sahara of today. Even the pyramids of Egypt may
have once surveyed a lush landscape.

Farther to the south, still on the continent of Africa, lies the
Kalahari Desert, whose moisture is stored in the frozen landscapes and
icebergs of Antarctica. Although smaller than the Sahara, it stretches
beyond the orbiter windows from the edge of the cold Atlantic in the
west to the limits of the eastern horizon. Like other deserts, its
moisture levels amount to less than 10 cm (4 in.) a year, but the
Kalahari supports a wonderful variety of wildlife, which survive on its
grasses and creeping plants. From space, its reddish soil is broken by
dusty white pockmarks, the salt residue from ancient evaporated lakes.
If you look closely, you can see the Okavango Delta, the greatest

*Man's
technology is
no match for
the forces of
nature in the
Sahara.*

Right: From space, the red sands of the Kalahari Desert appear to be covered with white holes. Years of drought have evaporated the water from lakes, leaving salt-encrusted patches on the landscape.

Inset: The sinewy fingers of the Okavango River delta in Botswana reach out into an area of the desert that once contained a prehistoric lake. Wildlife in this area of life-giving water is threatened by the conversion of their habitat to pastureland for domestic cattle.

inland river delta in the world. This unique formation stretches
outward like a hand, its fingers embedded in the surrounding desert.
Occasionally, an orbit may bring me over another unusual Kalahari
landmark, one that is as difficult to pronounce as it is to spell. The
Makgadikgadi salt pan is an intriguing remnant of this great lake
whose water evaporated, leaving a thick expanse of salt. Some areas

of this salt pan still receive moisture, but not enough to re-create a much-needed fresh water supply.

Another outstanding display of sand occurs in an area near and dear to the hearts of astronauts. White Sands, New Mexico, is an alternate landing site for the shuttle orbiter. Its dunes are composed of fine white grains of gypsum, which are blown from the broad bed of ancient Lake Lucero at the south end of the Tularosa Valley between the San Andres and Sacramento mountains.

Whenever wind collects sand or smaller particulates, they are redistributed over a large area on the surface of the Earth. A Saharan dust storm, for example, can be seen from space flight, sometimes as a distinct dust front, like a cloud, or even as a diffuse blurring of the geological features that are enveloped by it. More than 102 million t (100 million tons) of debris can be carried in these dust storms, which may fall far from their origin in places such as Paris, where snow is occasionally coloured by the red dust of the Sahara. On the shuttle, we don't need to worry about these storms clogging our equipment, because we are flying high above them. They would only be of concern if we encountered one while coming in for a landing at the Cape, but it is rare for such desert dust to reach Florida.

All the deserts I pass over are incredible areas of our world, where life-forms need to adjust constantly to temperature or to unpredictable moisture. As I unclamp the straw from my drink bag and feel the soothing lemonade on the back of my throat, the idea of water as a precious resource takes on a whole new meaning. One source of moisture, ocean fog, is easily photographed from space as it settles along the Atlantic coast of the Namib Desert. Cold water, known as the Benguela Current, flows from Antarctica north along the coast, creating this life-giving morning fog which provides moisture for the desert's diverse plant and animal population. Ironically, at the same time, it reduces the amount of rainfall, ensuring that the Skeleton Coast is worthy of its name and reputation.

Left: Lake Chad, Africa, in June 1966.

Right: Lake Chad in October 1992. In the past two decades, severe droughts have extensively reduced the surface area of the lake. In this photograph, the K'Yobe River, flowing into the lake on the northwest shore, has wetted the northern lake basin for the first time in several years.

Monitoring climate changes from space has, through the years, provided information on the state of the environment and hence the economy of many countries, especially those in sun-baked regions where water is scarcer than oil. One environmental marker is Lake Chad, a shared resource of four African countries — Nigeria, Niger, Chad, and Cameroon. Early in June 1966, *Gemini 9* astronauts photographed this lake, which was already shrinking due to the evaporation of floodwaters accumulated from the December and January rains. In the more than twenty years since that *Gemini* mission, Lake Chad has shrunk in size by 92 percent. The decline continues, in spite of favourable rains, and is an indicator of environmental changes occurring in the Sahel.

Even in Australia, the effects of heat and dryness are major factors in the evolution of a lake that drains one of the largest areas in the world. Lake Eyre can be spotted by astronauts in low Earth orbit. Its changing lake levels reflect back either a large water-filled basin or, more commonly lately, a salt pan with a central red eye. It is likely, given current predictions, that Australia will eventually suffer further desertification.

Like the desert, the forest areas of the world look serene and static from above. The human eye can't distinguish rainforests from temperate forests, or wetlands, nor are there any clues that it may take two hundred years for ancient trees — burned to make room for crops and pastureland or felled by loggers — to regrow in the old growth forests. The burning of the rainforests looks very passive from space. Pillars of smoke extend across to the horizon and, by their coverage of the land below, I can guess at the size and numbers of the fires. From each shuttle flight, photographs document changes along a famous Brazilian highway called BR364, part of the Polonoroeste Project, which is clearing land for development. Smoke now covers immense areas in the Amazon where before there were only small patches. Land that was once cloaked in mist is now choked in smoke.

Apart from the forests and wetlands, the coral reefs of the world are the largest living structure visible from space. They exist roughly below the orbital path of the lowest inclination flights of the shuttle (28.5 degrees north and south of the equator) and reach their greatest single accumulation in the Pacific Ocean, along the coast of Australia, where the Great Barrier Reef extends for more than 1930 km (1,200 mi.). Knowing that I cannot distinguish from space flight individual human beings or the structures they have built, it is hard to believe that when I gaze at the Great Barrier Reef, I am looking at something built by tiny

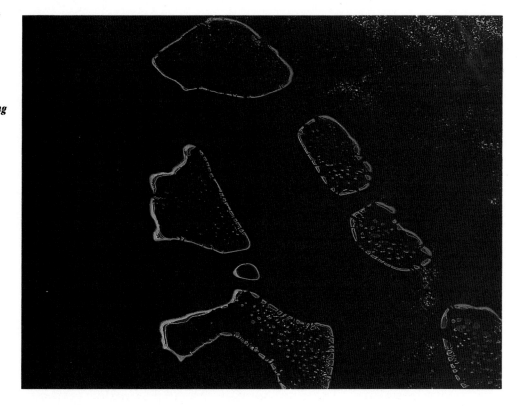

living creatures, whose babies are less than 2 mm in length. In this part of the world, these living organisms have covered 350 000 km^2 (135,146 sq. mi.) of ocean by producing 102 to 508 t (100 to 500 tons) of calcium carbonate per acre per year.

Many types of reefs have been described by researchers. Charles Darwin was the first to postulate, correctly, that reefs are formed around volcanic islands. The ancient volcanic islands of Raiatea and Tahaa of the Society Islands in the Pacific (see page 1) have an encircling reef structure, whereas in the Maldives, the volcanic islands have sunk below the surface of the Indian Ocean and only a ring of coral remains. The corals of the Maldives have been able to grow fast enough around the sinking islands to maintain contact with both the older, submerged reef and the surface of the ocean. They demonstrate the distinctive features of atolls. In the Great Barrier Reef, there are ribbon reefs up to 25 km (16 mi.) long and 500 m (1,640 ft.) wide. Of the more than two thousand continental islands off the coast of Australia, some seven hundred fifty of them have fringing reefs. Peering out the orbiter windows, I see these coral reefs as delicate rings, like footprints along the shores of eastern Australia. They are somewhat akin to icebergs; only a small proportion of the total structure is visible above the level of the sea.

I was taught in school that three-quarters of the Earth's surface is covered by water. It is difficult to put these numbers into proper perspective from space. There are so many irregular coastlines and bits of land scattered about the oceans that I can hardly conceive of anyone measuring accurately how much is water and how much is land. As we fly over the ocean, we sometimes can see wave-like patterns created by the shells of oceanic creatures deposited and built up on the seafloor. Submarine canyons slice into the sands in areas like the Great Bahama Bank southeast of Andros Island. Here the Tongue of the Ocean infiltrates the sands, carving marine canyons as deep as 3000 m (9,843 ft.). The Earth's crust is just as dynamic under the oceans as it is on land. In fact, the largest mountain range in the

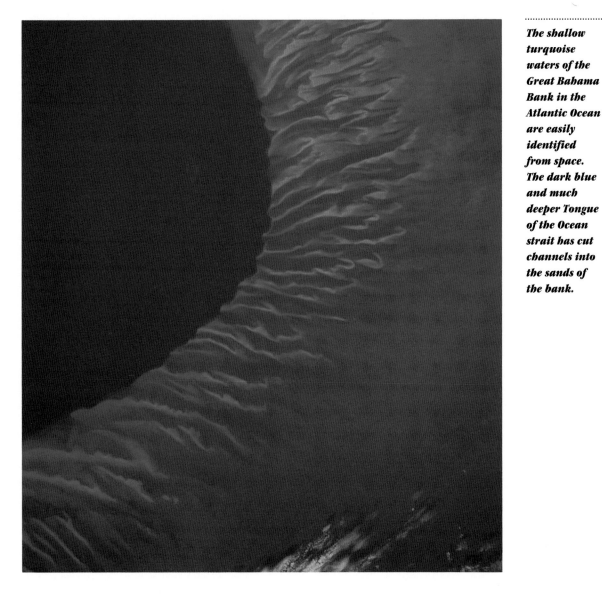

world, the Mid-Atlantic Ridge, is in the Atlantic Ocean, and the greatest depth is reached in the Mariana Trench in the Pacific Ocean.

We have learned a great deal about our planet in the short time we have been travelling above the atmosphere, and there is much more to learn. Interpreting satellite and shuttle imagery from space has enabled us to document changes in the continents and oceans. But it is also very important to recognize changes in the Earth with the human eye. When you see something with your own eyes, and unaided mind, changes become very real and very immediate.

Just as there are no political boundaries visible from space, there are no environmental boundaries either. I recognize that the outer crust of our planet is supporting the life-forms that can survive on it, or in it, with unique and finite resources. But it is important to remember that the planet itself will live on long after present-day life-forms have passed into history. Mankind will not stop evolution — although we may have a role in the direction and time it takes — because no matter how powerful *Homo sapiens* is as a species, the forces that change the outer crust and work continuously inside the heart of the planet are even more powerful. The Earth's crust will be beautiful whether there are human eyes to see it or not.

This is my last visual contact with the planet from orbit before I set forth in my exploratory pod to touch the Earth. I have witnessed wonders from space of which I know little or nothing. The things that were so clear to me before my launch are but faint memories of a scientific, fragmented, Earth-biased view. I feel the joy inside my entire

On January 30, 1992, **Discovery** touched down at Edward's Air Force Base in California.

body as I gently right myself in preparation for the last dive down through the access port between the mid-deck and flight deck. There are many practical tasks ahead before I smell the Earth again and am enclosed in that incredible blue cotton that I have seen from above for so many days.

The image of the bright blue atmosphere as a rainbow between the black universe and the sliding sheets of Earth's landscape stays with me as I complete my tasks. It seems to promise a pot of gold at its end, the likes of which I have never known. I promise myself that I will have adventure, love, and fun each day of my life. I will always think of the Earth as never before, cherishing the sense of awe that this flight has inspired within me. I cannot imagine what new dimensions of thought will surround my life's work, because of this moment in time. The Earth is ready for me, and I am ready for the Earth.

DISCOVERY/HOUSTON: BURN LOOKS GOOD. GOING OVER THE HILL. WILL TALK TO YOU ON THE OTHER SIDE AT TWO THREE.

DISCOVERY/HOUSTON: YOU LOOK ON ENERGY AT HACK INTERCEPT.

ROGER.

DISCOVERY/HOUSTON: YOU ARE ON GLIDESLOPE ON CENTERLINE. SURFACE WINDS ARE CALM.

ROGER.

HOUSTON/DISCOVERY: WHEEL STOP.

DISCOVERY/HOUSTON: ROGER, *DISCOVERY*, AND WELCOME BACK. YOUR MISSION HAS GIVEN US A PREVIEW OF SPACE-STATION OPERATIONS, AND A LOOK AT THE INTERNATIONAL COOPERATION THAT WILL BE A PART OF FUTURE SPACE EXPLORATION. IT'S A NICE JOB, RON.

THANKS, JOHN. WE SURE ALL ENJOYED IT.

ON PLANET EARTH

JANUARY 30, 1992

DISCOVERY/HOUSTON:
YOU HAVE A GO TO GET OUT OF THE SUITS.

THANKS, JOHN. WE'RE GETTING QUITE ATTACHED TO THEM
IN THE LITERAL SENSE.

Back from the future, the new phase of my life begins with my first, somewhat wobbly step on Earth. Where are the cameras to record this one small step that should be in my baby album? I can't help it. I am absolutely thrilled with the successful reentry and landing. Here I stand, actually on the surface of a planet. And not just any old planet. This is the most beautiful place around. No need here for life-support systems in the normal course of events. People are hugging me, and their touch is so welcome. Human contact is wonderful.

What amazing creatures we are, to develop the means to fly beyond that diffuse blue that now rests above me. There is not much time to reflect on my space-flight experience right now, though. There are medicals, postflight scientific testing, and the return air flight to Houston ahead of me.

I hope the photographs taken inflight capture the Earth as I remember seeing it — in a way I couldn't have imagined preflight. One of the first objects removed from the orbiter is the bag of film exposed throughout the mission. This film is returned to the Johnson Space Center, where it is processed and immediately duplicated. The original film is stored in nitrogen, and all slides and prints are made from at least a second generation film rather than from the original. This precaution avoids any chance of scratching the original emulsion.

The Earth observation personnel, using special magnifiers, try not to salivate excessively over the working copies of the inflight footage. Their first step is to select significant photographs for our press conference and for the official crew debrief, which takes about a month. Each Earth observation scientist chooses frames within his or her area of expertise to present mission-specific phenomena, such as Mount Pinatubo, in the context of photographs taken on previous space flights. The lessons learned from Earth observation on my mission, STS-42, will be discovered in the days, weeks, and months ahead, even after scientists are inundated with more exquisite photographs from the next mission.

This information will be presented to the scientific community in scientific journals. It will also be accessible to the public in the SSEOP catalogue system. Designed to catalogue all Earth observation shuttle photography, this computer program allows anyone to access space photographs by sorting through the pictures by flight number, roll number, longitude, latitude, or even geographical name or phenomena. The inflight cameras are not equipped to imprint onto the film the direction the camera was facing when a particular site was photographed. This has to be assigned to each picture by hand after the mission. When I use SSEOP, I can pick out the type of scene that I want, or at least exclude those that I don't want. For example, if I want the horizon in a photograph, I need to pick out only those pictures that are called "high oblique." This type of photograph is taken with the camera pointed up to include the horizon, whereas the pictures taken with the camera pointing away from the upright are called "low oblique." Even the amount of cloud cover in each frame is estimated as a percentage by the Earth observation ground support team. As technology evolves, these images will become more easily available to the general public. Currently, images from shuttle flights have been stored on video disks and are available from NASA.

The science experiments performed on my mission are, of course, the reason that I flew in space. The debriefs continue, hour by hour, about every system in *Discovery* and every experiment. The compulsion to share the whole adventure rather than just the technical aspect is overwhelming. For me, it seems natural to flip from the crisp language and definitions of science to the more philosophical language needed to describe the sometimes emotional events of the flight. My thoughts are centred around the glowing blue crystal ball called Earth. It is easy to forget that Earth is a planet. Most people are not consciously aware that we are travelling through a solar system. They may look up into the night sky and philosophize about life "out there," somewhere, moving through space, but life on their own planet seems static and stable, as though on a platform that is at the centre of creation. However, natural forces have always been at work on the Earth. In fact, evolution theory is predicated upon changes originating through such forces, and now there is the added dimension of changes brought about by people's intellect and activities. Like all human beings, I have inherited from previous generations the ability to cope with living upon a changing planet. Because my lifetime and goals are so much shorter than the time scale involved in the overall background redesigning of the Earth's crust, I always live in the hope that cataclysmic events "will not happen to me." Like most of my fellow Earth dwellers, I assume that avalanches, volcanoes, earthquakes, dust storms, and droughts will not directly affect my life, yet I know in my heart that someday they will greatly alter the lives of others.

The expression "one day at a time" appeared reasonable to me before space flight. The changes on the Earth's crust — from the building of the Rocky Mountains to the birth of volcanic islands — seemed to have slowed down or stopped for my life span. From time to time major events, such as the eruption of Mount St. Helens, made me rethink my relationship with the natural environment. However, after an initial few years of reading books and articles, this rethinking

Right: A computer-reconstructed picture of images of the moon and our home planet taken by the Galileo spacecraft from a distance of 6.2 million km (3.9 million mi.).

Inset: An environmentally friendly home in Denmark.

faded away in the wake of other events. The overwhelming expanse of the world, to me, was stable. I crave stability, just like anybody else. It's not often there for everyone, day to day, in our emotional lives, and, therefore, the physical environment seems to provide it.

Since my space flight, I have been reflecting upon and remoulding my preflight and inflight thoughts and perceptions. I need science, even more now, to help understand my relationship with this planet, which is of course not a static entity at all. In the history of human life on Earth, everyone plays a unique role in interfacing with the planet by just being here. Science helps us to understand the natural phenomena and complex interactions that affect us and, through technology, helps us to adapt to them. In a way, technology plays an important role in our evolution as a species. Other species evolve fairly rapidly compared to us, because their generation times are very short. Plants, for instance, with an average generation time of one year, produce many seeds. Since each seed's combination of genetic material is different, one seed is bound to grow regardless of what the climatic conditions are within a certain range. Humans, on the other hand, live much longer and only have relatively few prodigy, so we can't adapt as quickly to climatic change. Instead, we've developed houses and other products of technology to protect us from the elements; otherwise, we couldn't live in some of the places we do. Yet, at the same time that technology drives our evolution on the planet, it can suppress other life-forms that can't deal with our technological changes. We have, in effect, changed the evolutionary pattern of the planet as a whole.

When people place little emphasis on science in the school

Left: This photograph of the moon was taken by the Apollo 11 astronauts.

Centre: In this photograph taken on the moon, sunlight reflects off the surface of the Earth, creating a "crescent Earth."

Right: Future astronauts returning to the moon will find the lunar excursion module, the lunar rover, and the large dish antenna covered with lunar dust.

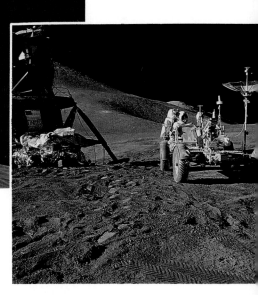

curriculum or in their lives in general, they are leaving to
someone else the responsibility of helping us understand,
cope with, and adapt to a changing environment. Science
is an ongoing learning experience, and the knowledge which it provides
can ease some of our fears about the future. Ironically, though, at the
same time that many of us reject science as being boring or irrelevant to
our lives, we view ourselves as being very sophisticated technologically.

The black-and-white scenes of the *Apollo 11* landing are part of my history and heritage. It was a beautiful experience seeing those images on television, and later in the evening of that historic July day in 1969, the moonlight touched me as never before. I was so proud of my species and this extraordinary accomplishment. However, today it's difficult to find consistent coverage of any launch of *Homo sapiens* into space. We have become quite indifferent about these technological achievements that are, in fact, still experimental. Video games and blue-screen effects in the movies distort the reality of what humans can actually do, and technology is assumed to be at a level that, has not yet been attained.

In addition, we often develop and use products of technology in an unthinking way. Sometimes out-of-date technology, produced in countries where resources are plentiful, is redistributed to poorer nations that are either unable to use it or unable to dispose of it. For example, older-model electric sewing machines have been sent to countries with few electrical facilities, and trains developed for use in temperate climates have been shipped to desert countries where they soon break down and are abandoned. In industrialized nations, technology is used to improve lifestyles, but future generations are endangered because of the inability to dispose of that same technology. In a perfect world, technology and a process to deal with it when it becomes obsolete would be developed at the same time. We have the ability to do that now. There are numerous examples, including metal shredders that shred old cars so that their metal can be reused, thus reducing the stockpile of rusty car parts. Fiscal and political issues can discourage reducing technology from happening on a larger scale, but public outcry can change this. One way all of us can begin to deal with this problem is to apply the 3 Rs — reduce, reuse, and recycle — to the products of technology that are part of our everyday lives. After all, we can't expect natural mechanisms, such as trees, to recycle the products of technology for us.

Science and technology are expected to make life on Earth better, but ultimately, it is the special relationship between humans and the environment that promotes our living in harmony with the changes that continue to take place upon the Earth's surface. Every generation has had a common goal: to be healthy and happy. And we have chosen to live in places that best suit these needs, although no perfect haven exists on Earth. The requirements for safe water, food, and air supplies will always remain a challenge.

After observing the planet for eight days from space, I have a deeper interest and respect for the forces that shape our world. Each particle of soil, each plant and animal is special. I also marvel at the creativity and ingenuity of our own species, but at the same time, I wonder why we all cannot see that we create our future each day, and that our local actions affect the global community, today as well as for generations to come. From the distance of space flight, it's easy to believe that we can live in harmony with one another and the environment. It's important, though, that we all share this view, not just the few Earthlings who fly in space. Young people, in particular, need good role models so that they understand the importance of an environmental ethic. We must not thrust upon children the responsibility of saving the environment. We are all involved.

In our schools, respect for other individuals and other cultures should be taught hand-in-hand with respect and caring for our ecosystem. The strong sense of bonding that develops when individuals work together as a team also occurs in the depths of space, in a thin piece of metal hurtling at more than twenty-five times the speed of sound. In space, where there were no other life-forms aside from my fellow crew members, I felt the strength of those we had left behind on the planet. As part of an intricate and complex life system, we should not have any difficulty in conceiving that other people, and other life-forms, are as important to us as we are to ourselves.

Generally, the behaviour of most species is predictable. The variations in behaviour within *Homo sapiens*, however, are extraordinary. This dynamic aspect of human nature, as unnerving as it may seem sometimes, is as important as our technology in terms of adaptability. Cultural diversity is another way we ensure our survival on this planet. Throughout the world, our uniqueness has been shaped by powerful natural forces, and different cultures have developed different ways of dealing with the environment. What we do in North America doesn't necessarily work somewhere else. It is

Left: Ceremonies at the 1992 Olympics in Barcelona, Spain.

Right: These handmade bags from Quito, Ecuador, reflect an ancient craft tradition that makes them attractive to other cultural groups that rely on technology for such goods.

this ability to look at a problem from many different perspectives that sets us apart from other animals. We have great potential for survival as a species if we pool our ideas and creativity and understand that our diversity is beneficial to us as fellow Earthlings. A joy for living can be the best common bond among us.

Whenever I visit new places around the world, I find it hard to believe that I did not know before that such a place or such peoples existed. We seem to know so little about other lands and the other dwellers on our home planet. Since my flight into space, though, I find myself wanting to explore as much of Earth as possible. I have a need to use my senses to make each new place a reality for me. The two-dimensional pictures that adorn the books on my travel bookshelves are reflections of other adventurers, seen through eyes other than my own. To see the pyramids in Egypt with the dust in my eyes and throat, or to make my way through a rainforest, emotionally bonds me with those places and makes them a real part of my life. Visiting people in other lands makes them part of my reality, too. (It seems odd, after having looked upon countries with no restrictions from space, to have to worry now about visas and passports. When I was told that I could not visit the Aswan High Dam in Egypt because it was a military area, I wanted to protest, "But I've just flown over it! I've taken pictures of it from space!")

Long ago, small pockets of human population affected their local environment to some extent. But it is only recently that the accumulated biomass of mankind has affected the global environment. Our basic requirements of water, food, and a place to live have driven civilization to spread itself well beyond the fragile communities that were sufficient for early man. We should not feel guilty that we have these basic requirements, but we need to try to understand them, and put them in the context of all the other life-forms that interact with us and with the planet. The demands of our society are becoming increasingly complex, promoting caring, on the one hand, and encouraging an overwhelming desire for economic or political power on the other. Regardless of these social developments, including our tendency to cluster into cities, our basic requirements have not changed from the days of our prehistoric ancestors. What has changed are our numbers and our use of both land and water to satisfy these requirements.

Not long ago, I read that a scientist had postulated that *Homo sapiens* is halfway through its life span as a species upon Earth. This type of prediction can be extrapolated from figures obtained in studying faster-growing life-forms, such as bacteria, and the rate at which they utilize the natural resources around them. I hope that enough of us are aware of population and environmental issues to make a change and reverse what appears, at least on paper, to be a most unpleasant future for upcoming generations. Mind you, there are many astounding facts about our species that are undeniable, such as approximately 200 million new babies born per year. However, there are also positive signs that change is occurring. In Thailand, in less than three decades, the average birth rate has dropped from 6.2 to 2.2 births. This dramatic drop can be attributed largely to the work of the Thailand National Family Planning Program, which oversees a national network of eight thousand government facilities offering family-planning facilities.

The pressure on the planet's resources to sustain our continually expanding population increases by the minute. Our need for fresh water over the past three centuries has multiplied by more than thirty-five times, especially recently, with the demands of industry and personal convenience. The importance of water to humans cannot be underestimated. Like the Earth's surface, human bodies are made up

In this colour infrared photograph of the Island of Hawaii, forested areas are dark red; cultivated land, lighter red and pink; sparse vegetation on volcanic summits, green-grey; and recent lava flows, black. Sugarcane (above), which requires large amounts of water, is cultivated along the northern shore.

mostly of water, which resides inside each living cell. Without water, a human being cannot live very long. In the orbiter, the water supply includes a potable stored supply plus water as a by-product of the fuel cells. Adding iodine to the water supplies helps ensure that there will not be any sickness in space that is due to the presence of another Earth life-form to which humans are not accustomed, or with which human life is incompatible.

Back on Earth, oceans account for 97.2 percent of the global water inventory. The 2.15 percent that is locked up in glacial ice does not leave much fresh water for human use. Most cities cannot acquire enough water for sanitation, waste collection, and health services, let alone for drinking. Political boundaries place 230 million people in at least twenty-six countries where water can scarcely meet daily requirements. Compounding this problem for many countries is the vicious cycle of war and famine.

All the ocean water around Africa, for example, doesn't help the majority of its population. In industrialized countries, drinking untreated water or not washing our hands may seem repulsive, but this is a way of life in areas in Africa faced with the lack of a safe water supply. With much of the continent's fresh water locked up in the gigantic ice sheets of Antarctica, there has been talk of towing icebergs from there to provide this much-needed, life-giving liquid. Economically privileged countries, such as Saudi Arabia and Kuwait, are able to afford desalination plants to provide drinking water, but this process is three to four times more expensive than purifying conventional sources of fresh water. If desalination is to become a viable and environmentally sound method of providing potable water for more people, we will need to invent better methods of supplying energy for it.

Aquifers, which trap groundwater, sometimes for thousands of years, are another source of fresh water. Shallow aquifers occur in sand and gravel, producing a low yield of water that is rapidly replenished if it rains; however, aquifers deep down in the ground hold fossil water that has been present for perhaps as long as ten thousand years and is no longer being replenished as it is used. This water is like money in the bank, but once that money is gone, it's gone forever. It is unlikely that many of us think about how old the water is that comes out of a faucet, or where the source is located, but perhaps we should.

In North America, the largest store of groundwater in the world, the Ogallala aquifer, is situated from the southern part of South Dakota down midway into Texas, and from Wyoming through Colorado, Kansas, and Oklahoma, as far as New Mexico. This great resource is being depleted ten thousand times faster than it is being replenished. Twenty percent of all the irrigated land in the United States receives water from this vast store. Fortunately, farmers and politicians have now put conservation plans into effect.

Across the desert areas of the world, interesting circular structures have appeared in recent years, which from space resemble green measles spread across the red or light browns of the surrounding desert. These circles, varying from a few hundred metres to two to three kilometres in diameter, represent areas around water wells in which crops are grown. Groundwater is raised from depths of 500 m (1,640 ft.) and pumped through a horizontal pipe that moves around the well, spraying water over underlying crops. The underlying groundwater is being tapped like diamonds from a great depth in the

Left: The dark spots in this photograph of northern Saudi Arabia are thousands of agricultural fields in the desert. By the year 2000, the aquifers supplying them with water may almost be depleted.

Right: A close-up of the Jabal Tuwayq Irrigation Region in Saudi Arabia.

Inset: A pivot irrigation machine in New Mexico.

Earth's crust. This water is used for both domestic and agricultural purposes, but at a tremendous cost. The levels of evaporation in the desert are so high that much of the sprayed water evaporates before it reaches the ground. At current utilization rates in Saudi Arabia, the underground aquifer supplying the bulk of these irrigation projects will be unuseable by the year 2000. Future shuttle flights will record the disappearance of the "green measles" as the desert wind covers them with sand. (Surprisingly, these pivot irrigation systems can also be found in formerly forested areas of Brazil and Nicaragua, where rainfall has been reduced. Without trees, little water is returned to the air, and without clouds, no new rain falls.)

The need for water to supply electrical energy almost matches the need for water for agricultural purposes. Water is used directly to generate hydroelectric power, and indirectly as a coolant for electrical generators. The building of thousands of dams worldwide for these and other purposes has changed the natural course of rivers and landscapes forever. One of the largest attempts at reconstructing the surface of the Earth for the benefit of mankind, and one that is watched carefully from space on each shuttle flight, is the Aswan High Dam in Egypt. This dam and its 500 km (310-mi.)-long reservoir were designed to control floods that were devastating to human habitation along the Nile, and to alleviate famine-producing droughts by ensuring a steady water supply for three crops per year.

The Nile's delta is very old. Between 6000 B.C. and 5000 B.C., the

Left: A photograph taken in 1965 of the river Nile before the construction of the High Dam at Aswan.

Right: Lake Nasser was created when the dam was built.

Inset: At the top of the photograph, the Nile supplies water

for land irrigation projects. Domestic animals are

fed plants on the desert, only a short distance from the river.

fine mud that is characteristic of the delta was deposited there by the Nile at a rate of more than 10 million t (10 million tons) of silt and clay per year. By 5000 B.C. enough soil had accumulated to support farming by the early Egyptians. Most of the country's agriculture occurs within the triangle-shaped delta, whose base lies upon the

Mediterranean and whose apex reaches 160 km (100 mi.) south to Cairo. At the moment, the widest part of the delta stretches roughly 200 km (135 mi.) from east to west.

Photographs taken during *Gemini* missions in September and November 1966 captured the Nile and its delta before the construction of the new Aswan Dam. Since that time, successive shuttle flights have photographed the fluctuating water levels of Lake Nasser throughout the post-dam era. A build-up of silt, which cannot traverse the dam to reach the mouth of the Nile, will become more visible as time goes by in the southern part of the lake. Because no new sediment is reaching the delta area, by the year 2100, over 15 percent of the delta could disappear. The intricate balance between sediment, salt, and water in the delta is also changing as seawater infiltrates low-lying areas, causing the soil to become water-logged and more saline. Increased salinity of the water-logged mouth of the Nile means that the delta will not continue to be the rich agricultural area it was in the past. Egyptian farmers are now compelled to apply artificial fertilizer to compensate for the decline in nutrient-rich sediments that were deposited when the Nile flooded its banks.

There have been other problems as well. Fewer nutrients now reach the Mediterranean, with the result that the total fish catch diminished by one-third in the six-year period after the dam was built. Sardine fisheries in the eastern Mediterranean saw a 97 percent decrease in their catches. Farther upstream in the still reservoir,

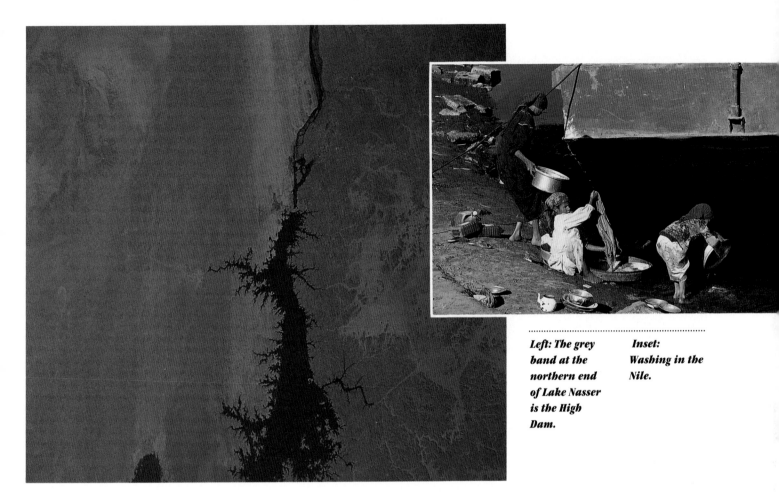

Left: The grey band at the northern end of Lake Nasser is the High Dam.

Inset: Washing in the Nile.

parasites that can infect humans are on the rise, as are mosquitoes that transport malaria. The river bed is gradually being eroded without the addition of new sediments, and even the Aswan Dam itself is not untouched — weeds and rotting debris are constantly sucked into the turbines. These problems are unlikely to disappear in the near future.

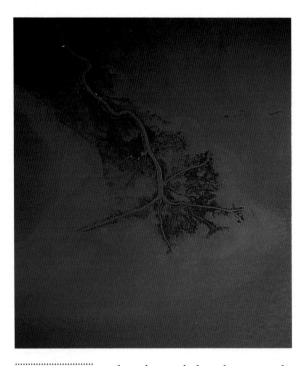

The Mississippi River delta, a major habitat for wildlife, is threatened by efforts to control the river with flood levees and canals. The dark areas between the channels are marshes.

Dams have also had a major impact on the North American landscape. In 1935 the large Hoover Dam was built in Arizona, and since then, more than two thousand major dams have been constructed across rivers to meet the need for a secure water supply, electricity, irrigation, and recreation. The once-mighty Colorado River, which carved the Grand Canyon thousands of years ago, is no longer allowed to flow unimpeded to the Gulf of California. Close to the Colorado's mouth, near the Mexican border, salt levels exceeding 1,500 parts per million are high enough to kill plants. And industrial wastes have made the water in the Grand Canyon toxic.

Even the mighty Mississippi has been "tamed" by flood levees and canals that run up and down the river to facilitate navigation. The more than 29 000 km (18,000 mi.) of canals, created to provide access to oil fields, allow seawater from the Gulf of Mexico to flood back into the Mississippi Delta. The land shrinks further as oil and gas supplies are removed. Recreational activities chew away at the soft canal banks, and 145 km^2 (56 sq. mi.) of wetlands are lost every year because sediments can no longer reach these areas, whose productivity depends upon rich silt and fresh water.

The gradual shrinking of the Aral Sea in Eastern Europe, recorded over the years in shuttle photographs, is another striking example of human intervention. More than thirty years ago, large-scale diversion schemes enabled about 10 million ha (25 million a.) to be irrigated in Uzbekistan and Turkmenistan. Formerly, the two rivers, Syrdar'ya in the northeast and the Amudar'ya in the south, spilled large quantities of sediment as well as water downstream, thereby continuously enlarging their deltas. The Aral Sea was once the fourth-largest lake in the world. After the diversion of water to the numerous irrigation projects in 1960, water levels in the lake dropped by nearly 12 m (40 ft.), reducing the lake by a third of its original area.

With this drop in water levels, the salinity of the Aral Sea has nearly tripled, and salt-encrusted soils are now found as far as 100 km (62 mi.) inland. Twenty species of fish have since become extinct, wiping out the jobs of more than sixty thousand local inhabitants. The former seaports of Aral'sk and Muynak are now located 32 and 22 km (20 and 14 mi.) inland. Winds whip up the salt and dump it onto adjacent agricultural lands at the rate of 48 million t (47 million tons) per year. Without the moderating effect of the larger lake, the growing season has been reduced by at least ten days over an area stretching 200 km (124 mi.) from the water's edge. Agriculture now requires massive amounts of fertilizers, pesticides, and herbicides, and the drinking water has become contaminated by them. Respiratory and eye problems have increased in the local population as a result of the airborne salt. In addition, boars, deer, and egrets have vanished from the area.

In 1990, an agreement between the United Nations and the U.S.S.R. Environment Program underscored the need for international action to save the Aral Sea. To do so will require tremendous infusions of money — not easily available in today's economy. Time will tell

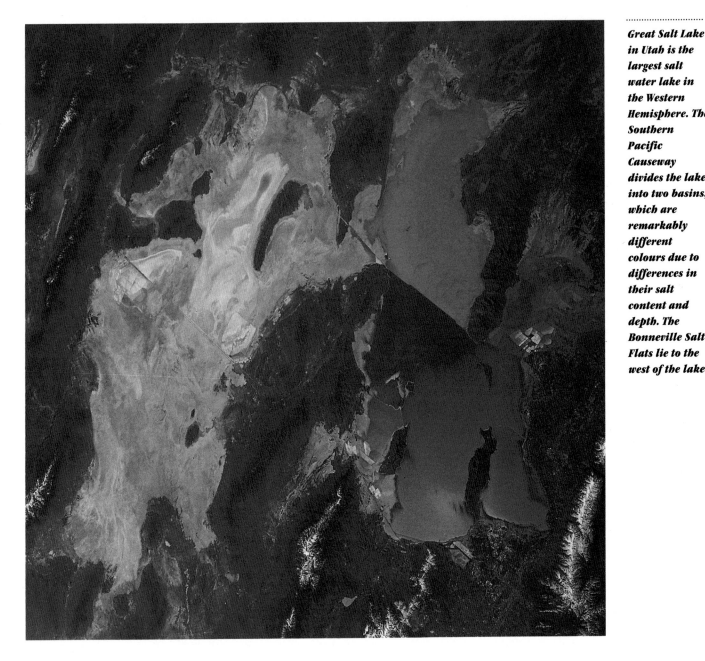

Great Salt Lake in Utah is the largest salt water lake in the Western Hemisphere. The Southern Pacific Causeway divides the lake into two basins, which are remarkably different colours due to differences in their salt content and depth. The Bonneville Salt Flats lie to the west of the lake.

whether or not this lake will disappear from the maps of the world.

We are at a crossroads in understanding the benefits and drawbacks of building dams and diverting water for various irrigation projects. One of the most powerful dams on the face of the Earth will be built in China if the Three Gorges Project goes ahead as planned. The diversion of 1190 km (740 mi.) of water from the Yangtze River, near Shanghai, would flood 24 280 ha (60,000 a.) of farmland and displace nearly 1.2 million people in order to generate 20 percent of China's energy needs. The 183 m (600 ft.) dam will create a 595 km (370-mi.)-long lake on the Yangtze River. The increasing population of China, the small amount of arable land, and the demand for hydroelectric power in the drive for a more westernized lifestyle have increased the number of dams in the country from 2 in 1950 to well over 36,500 by the mid-1980s. The displacement of people and the loss of traditional lands and lifestyles are large factors in the decision of international organizations to withdraw financial support for large dam projects worldwide.

In Canada, a mammoth hydroelectric project on James Bay is under close scrutiny. Fortunately, it is being constructed in phases. With the first phase complete, a variety of groups are now looking at the horrendous environmental impact of flooding vast areas in northwestern Quebec, and are trying to determine whether the rest of the project should go ahead. Caribou migration routes have been disrupted, fish spawning grounds destroyed, native people displaced, and local lands, used for hunting and fishing, flooded. The suddenly unleashed water has released quiescent industrial wastes such as mercury into the food chain. As well, the fragile ecosystem where fresh and salt water meet has been disrupted, with adverse effects on marsh grasses, migratory birds, and large mammals such as beluga whales and polar bears.

In the future, when dams or other irrigation projects are being planned, we should insist that scientists and engineers provide policy makers with up-to-date environmental information so that a long-term vision can be developed that takes into consideration the concerns of indigenous people and the consequences of each specific undertaking. Projects that appear to be wonderful in the present can compound the very problems they were meant to solve, in the future.

Another way that we damage our planet's lakes and rivers is by using them for sewage disposal. One such lake is located high in the plateau of the Altiplano in South America. Lake Titicaca, the world's highest navigable lake, is the reported birthplace of the Inca culture, and today is shared by Peru and Bolivia. From 1940 to 1990, the population of Puno, on the Peruvian shores of the lake, increased one hundred-fold in the city and immediate surrounding area. The lack of financial resources to provide careful urban planning or sewage treatment technology resulted in the introduction of untreated sewage into this Andean lake. In the mid-1980s, the area was blessed with rains, causing flooding that slowed some of the build-up in the lake of excessive nutrient enrichment caused by the sewage. Unfortunately, high population densities and the health problems created by deteriorating water conditions and food supplies are not exceptions in our developing world.

The need for proper disposal of sewage and garbage is an increasing concern as old methods of landfill and dumping at sea catch up with us. These methods have even resulted in the extinction of a species (although one that some would say won't be missed). On St. Helena, an island off the Atlantic Coast of Africa, a garbage dump attracted a great many mice. They are considered to be the reason behind the extinction of the world's largest wingless earwig (*Labidura herculeana*), last spotted in 1965. These not-so-little creatures (about 8 cm/3 in.) couldn't escape from the much bigger, quicker, and toothier mice.

Inside the orbiter, where everything floated, dealing with garbage was a very tricky business. Thankfully, the trash was not dumped into space, where it would float around above us or be the source of a "debris strike" to some other unsuspecting shuttle or satellite. Spacecraft today are not great at recycling, but reusing is at least one environmental "R" that is adopted.

Through the window of the orbiter, sunlight reflecting off the surface of the ocean sometimes picked up the traces of ships that had passed by days before. These ships still dump nonbiodegradable plastic into what some people consider to be the infinite reservoir of the ocean. It is estimated that each North American generates about 1.8 kg (4 lb.) of trash per day on average. This mountain of garbage includes biodegradable waste, some of which doesn't break down as rapidly in landfills as was previously thought. Even on Mount Everest, explorers and Sherpas are now picking up the more than 51 t (50 tons) of garbage left by previous achievers of the summit.

Of course, it is easy to look in retrospect at mankind's activities and point fingers, but do we really know what mirror we'll face in the future? Sometimes, the combination of human activities with the normal, natural effects of the environment inadvertently result in great destruction. In the Galapagos Islands of Ecuador, feral goats ate most of the greenery from Barrington Island at a time when there was a slight change in climate. The combination of these two factors is thought to be responsible for the loss of the vermilion flycatcher and the large tree finch from this area. Although the introduction of domestic animals may have been well intentioned if naive in many areas of the world, other actions have been driven by the desire to obtain money at the expense of other animal life-forms. In 1989 the United Nations Convention on International Trade and Endangered Species (CITES) placed a total ban on all trade in ivory, because of the decline in the population of the African elephant. The state of the black rhino is even worse; only three thousand remain today compared to sixty thousand just fifteen years ago. Unfortunately, generating wealth is often at the expense of the other creatures that share the planet with us and at the expense of the system that provides us with life-giving food and water.

The tremendous variability of Earth's environment, in terms of altitude, climate, and moisture conditions, results in an extraordinary diversity of living plant and animal material, known as biodiversity. The interaction and interdependence of a variety of life-forms, rather than the number of one type of life-form, is essential to the ecosystem. The study of an ecosystem, whether it be the desert, the rainforest, coral reefs, or the ocean, creates an accumulation of knowledge imparted by countless human beings through many generations. This is very important because human sensitivity to interacting ecosystems is the key to successfully integrating humans with Earth's other unique inhabitants.

Quite often, both from my views of it from space and from visits on the ground, the desert gives the impression of being a large, dry environment without life. In fact, the desert is an interweaving of many microenvironments, each in constant flux, in which organisms have a small range of flexibility to adjust to the dynamic forces at work. For example, desert life-forms have to be very resistant to extremes in temperature — cold temperatures by night and hot temperatures by day. Plants and animals have also evolved to cope with sandblasting winds, infrequent drops of moisture, and the baking rays of the sun. Some plants may not be seen for decades until a long-awaited rain coaxes them out of a dream-time state to blossom and

Left: The linear sand dunes of the Namib Desert are framed by the ocean and the flatter desert terrain.

Inset: Crescent-shaped sand dunes in the Sahara may seem devoid of life, but contain micro-environments.

Above: The yucca, a desert plant, is used by indigenous people for clothing, by veterinarians as a medication, and by animals and birds for shelter and food.

enter the complex ecosystem, albeit briefly. To conserve water, desert animals produce very concentrated urine, and some larger animals keep cool heads with special blood vessels at the base of their brains. Desert spiders and birds, rattlesnakes and lizards are creatures that love it where they live, because they would not survive elsewhere.

Were it not for the biodiversity of small desert plants and animals, desert areas would be unsuitable for habitation by people and other large life-forms. However, overcropping and overgrazing remove the natural plants that anchor the drifting sand. In the Kalahari Desert, the effects of introduced cattle have been detrimental to the land and its indigenous wildlife. Huge fences built to contain the herds and prevent the spread of hoof-and-mouth disease have obstructed the natural migration of thousands of wildebeests. In times of extreme drought, when local patches of rain can no longer provide enough water and foliage for their daily requirements, wildebeest herds seek out permanent water bodies in the north. An estimated fifty thousand of these graceful animals died after they made their way along the Kuke fence to reach a well-known watering area, only to find it already trampled and depleted by cattle.

Animals in the desert have evolved to cope with the climate but have not been able to evolve quickly enough to cope with the technology we have thrust upon them. This is not to say that everyone must become a vegetarian. A short-term goal of a hamburger, however, multiplied by the world's population that has access to one, produces long-term effects on animal and plant life-forms, and on the soil upon which, ultimately, we all depend for our survival. In the past, nomadic herders and their families moved with the season in a sustainable relationship with their environment. This low-intensity activity of the past contrasts with today's high-intensity rearing of cattle that cannot survive if they stray very far from water or grass.

Mining is another human activity that has had an impact on the desert. The extraction of diamonds, for example, requires large quantities of water. Unfortunately, one of the largest diamond pipes in the world, the Orapa Diamond Mine, is located in the Kalahari, where water is as precious as diamonds.

As overcropping and overgrazing continue, in combination with climate changes that may or may not be compounded by human activity, more land will be converted to deserts and the deserts we know now will be in danger of losing some of their biodiversity. The destruction of desert environments does not evoke the same emotion among the public in general as does the destruction of lush rainforests. However, after the Gulf War, the fragility of the desert was movingly apparent to those trying to mop up the devastating effects of oil spills, airborne soot, and kilometres of tracks from both military equipment and personnel.

The greatest biodiversity on our planet resides in our disappearing rainforests, where more varieties of species reside per square metre than anywhere else on Earth. In contrast to temperate forests, which

The rainforest ecosystem has filled a niche in poor soil areas around the equator. The thick humus soil associated with the forest floors of temperate woodlands is not a feature of the rainforest.

may be the home of ten to thirty species of trees, there may be well over one hundred species in the same relative area of tropical forest. Before appreciating the life in the verdant rainforest canopy above, it is necessary to look down on the ground to ensure that one foot is being placed in front of the other without trodding on anyone. The floor of the rainforest is as active as the trunks of its trees, leaves, and vines, and the heavy air is filled with the dense perfume of exotic creatures and decaying organisms.

The multitude of exquisite, interacting life-forms in the rainforest has developed so much of its own complex technology that human

Left: In the northwestern corner of Madagascar, the Betsiboka River carries red soil from the land into the sea. Deforestation of the forests has led to tremendous soil loss.

Above: In this photograph taken in Ecuador, the mountain slopes have been stripped of large trees.

achievements pale in comparison. Various proteins, fats, waxes, hormones, drugs, sugars, amino acids, and fragrances are produced through the efficient use of solar energy to manufacture simple sugars from carbon dioxide. The number of creatures that are specialized to perform a single task should also be staggering to any human being. For instance, ants in the rainforest and elsewhere may not be as charismatic as some endangered species, and by their own number are not endangered themselves, but their importance in cleaning up the world cannot be underestimated. Coasting around the Earth in space, I couldn't have imagined plants that have developed special hormones to keep an insect in its juvenile state, or at the other extreme, to promote premature aging as a natural means of pest control. Even the viscous secretions of rubber compounds in leaves can gum up the jaws of the most persistent insect pest.

Three-fifths of the world's total rainforests are located in South and Central America, Southeast Asia, and West and Central Africa. It has been estimated that one-fifth to one-third of the original tropical forests in the world have already been lost. Although the deforestation of the Amazon declined somewhat in 1993, it is still proceeding at an alarming rate. Once the trees are gone, the soil is revealed for what it really is — barren. In a temperate forest, the soil contains organic material down to relatively decent depths. This is not the case in the tropical rainforest. I just have to clear away a few leaves on the forest floor to uncover unproductive ground covered by a matrix of roots that rest above it. Only the complex life-forms of the rainforests have been able to convert such land into a thing of grand design. It is unlikely that any other life-forms can use this land more efficiently. Certainly we cannot.

I may never in my lifetime be able to grasp the full significance of the rainforests' destruction. These unique ecosystems are laboratories where we can study and learn about organisms that occur nowhere else in our solar system, and, until proven otherwise, nowhere else in the universe. They are not just there to clean air polluted by industrialized countries. Rainforests provide us with drugs that combat high blood pressure and provide remission from leukemia and breast cancer. Currently, less than 1 percent of rainforest plants have been investigated as possible medical cures.

Not only tropical rainforests are in need of protection. The temperate rainforests of North America's west coast are being clear-cut and three-quarters of the forests in Europe have been damaged by sulphur deposits and acid rain generated by industry. After clearing temperate forest areas, the land is only useful if crop rotation is initiated. If this does not happen, chemical fertilizers are necessary. The effect on the ecosystem of using fertilizers is obvious in lakes, where excessive nutrients leaking from fields into the water stimulate

Above: The outlines of volcanic calderas are clearly visible from space on the seahorse-shaped island of Isabela and the smaller island of Fernandina in the Galapagos.

Inset: An eruption cloud drifts away from the Fernandina Volcano in the Galapagos Islands.

Above: Sally Lightfoot crabs dance over lava rocks to the sea while a marine iguana searches for a vegetarian meal.

the growth of algae and other plants, such as water hyacinth. In an ecosystem, nothing can replace the activity of a tree as a nutrient pump that recycles elements in the air, water, and soil.

More widely distributed than forests on all continents and in all latitudes is a diverse biosphere known under the general heading of

A marine iguana faces the sun and raises the front half of its body to maximize the amount of heat it can absorb from the sun's rays.

This Galapagos land iguana, which is larger and more colourful than its marine counterpart, rests in the brush.

"wetlands," but locally and scientifically as bog, moor, fen, and muskeg. Wetlands regulate water flows and sequester over 508 billion t (500 billion tons) of carbon dioxide in plant tissue. We are lucky on Earth to have so many natural "lungs." If these plants were burned or their habitats drained, the carbon dioxide would be released into the atmosphere.

Throughout the millennia, biodiversity has been, and continues to be, responsible for the widespread distribution and success of many plants and animals. The Galapagos Islands are famous, because they are unique ecosystems. Even with the best survival techniques, man could not have colonized these volcanic islands before other life-forms turned the barren rock and surrounding oceans into a mildly hospitable environment. To this day, because of the lack of fresh water on many of the small islands, people are still faced with great difficulty surviving there, whereas some plants and animals live quite

Left: The Galapagos penguin is the only penguin species that lives north of the equator.

Right: The blue-footed booby is adapted to nesting on the ground while

the red-footed booby nests in trees and shrubs.

happily in these locales.

Every shuttle mission flies over these islands, because their geographic location hugs the equator. A telephoto lens enables astronauts to take photographs of recent lava flows whose barren slopes contrast with older flows that are now inhabited by plants. Vegetation is scarce in the Galapagos, whose arid climate slows down the formation of soil from rock. The patches of vegetation appear green at ground level, but not from high above.

The position of the Galapagos, west of their mother country of Ecuador and far from the nearest Pacific island, resulted in a slow colonization by life-forms that had to either fly, float, or perhaps even swim to these harsh distant shores. The remoteness and isolation of these islands and the difficulty in colonizing them are reflected in the five hundred species native to the Galapagos compared to more than ten thousand on the mainland of Ecuador. According to current scientific theory, the islands' native plants and animals are the successful offspring of the original colonizers. Were it not for the combination of short generation times and a large genetic pool providing options for each species, this could have been the end of the evolutionary trail for any one of the founding members of the Galapagos ecosystem. The constant infusion of life from incoming tides encouraged natural selection of organisms that could quite happily live and thrive upon the new land. Visiting these islands, I am filled with a sense of wonder at the successes that one million years of colonization, isolation, and evolution have amassed. These plants and animals vary in their distribution and adaptation to differing micro-climates and other conditions with the result that many species endemic to the Galapagos are often endemic only to a specific island. The red-footed booby, for example, is common only on Tower and San Cristobal islands, and the flightless cormorant only on Fernandina and Isabela islands.

Mangroves, which can withstand the toxic effects of salt, stabilize shorelines and provide shelter for marine creatures. Coastal development has taken its toll on these unique ecosystems.

The Galapagos, which are now a national park and nature reserve, give me hope that life is always in the air and in the water, perhaps coming from distant lands, but always settling on or below some surface of the Earth to survive and maintain a lifehold on the planet. This symbolizes the ability of life on Earth to continue and to survive.

After my space flight and my visits to the desert, the rainforest, and the Galapagos Islands, it was important for me to dip my feet in the ocean, to interact with this vast resource. When I go to the ocean now, though, it is with the realization that when we fish, boat, or play in the sea, we must do it with a clear understanding of how our actions affect the ocean's life cycle.

Many environmental problems, man-made in origin, are associated with these great bodies of water. First, coastal development for tourism and for industry is taking its toll. Dunes, which protect beach areas, have been levelled, and mangroves, which trap sand and provide nutrients for fish and other sea creatures, have been cut down. Second, the sea and the coastline are still used as dump sites. Of course, circling Earth, visitors from another planet would not be able to appreciate at first glance that any of these problems were insurmountable, given the volume of the oceans. It is this process of thought, no doubt, that has propelled mankind along our current, destructive path.

The ocean is the single largest source of animal protein in the world, with two-thirds of the total catch from the Pacific alone. We need to understand that overfishing can push species beyond their recovery capability or affect other organisms in the food chain. Overfishing near the Shetland Islands caused upwards of forty-eight thousand puffin chicks to starve to death when the fish supply dropped. On the shores of resource-rich Canada, the codfishing industry has collapsed, with fish stocks and jobs disappearing. Improvements in technology — larger boats, sonar equipment to locate fish schools, and improved, stronger nets — have increased the catch, but creatures in the ocean have not been able to evolve fast enough to cope with this technology, and it is unlikely that they ever will. Even the cold, isolated continent of Antarctica is not safe from evolving technology, which enables the processing and canning of krill, a little shrimp-like creature, at rates of 135 kg (300 lb.) per hour. All nations should ensure that entrapment of any animal for human use is done in a sustainable manner, so that the resource is replenished at the same rate as it is withdrawn.

One of the most obvious effects of our travels upon the ocean is oil pollution. Who can forget images of wildlife covered in oil spilled from the *Exxon Valdez* in Prince William Sound, Alaska? More recently, the Gulf War polluted another fragile ecosystem with oil. The Persian Gulf itself is very shallow, requiring at least three years for water to circulate completely. It is lined by salt marshes, lagoons, coral reefs, and mangrove forests. In the initial oil spills, tens of thousands of birds were killed in the salt marshes, when their wings became matted with

In the aftermath of the Persian Gulf War, smoke from burning oil wells drifts across Kuwait.

oil. Other birds landed in reflecting pools in the desert, only to discover, too late, that the pools were filled with oil, not water.

The last of the oil wells that were set ablaze or uncapped in the war was extinguished in November 1991, but the effects of both airborne soot and water-borne oil will be felt for many years. The fragile desert, with such a small variety of life-forms, couldn't cope with this sudden event that had no precedent in the natural environment. From rather tranquil photographs of the Persian Gulf before the war, through point light sources of fires in the Gulf, to the postwar smoke, soot, and oil, space photography provided a historic record of a most unpleasant time in mankind's ascent — some would say descent — on planet Earth.

With the view from space showing so much ocean around our planet, seeing the Great Barrier Reef is very exciting for astronauts — evidence of life amidst the unbroken, smooth blue sheet that fills the spacecraft's windows. Coral reefs existed long before humans or most modern-day plants and animals appeared on the planet. Although the diversity of life-forms in the reefs has allowed these structures to be successful even during a few of the dark periods in the millennia of evolution, they have not always been as biologically diverse as they are today. Two billion years ago, algae formed the early reefs, and only 600 million years ago were sponges added. Following the collapse of one reef, there was a wave of reef building 488 million years ago, which improved the structure's resiliency by adding calcareous skeletons. Coral reefs have managed to survive three collapses, and the reefs that exist today have been hanging on for the past 10 million years.

When I have the opportunity to visit coral reefs, I am careful not to touch these beautiful sea creatures as I drift above them. I know my very presence is an invasion of an ecosystem that would need time for us to adapt to each other. It is the home of many plants and animals, and is in as intricate a balance with the sea as the rainforest is with the land. Visits to the reefs are important educational events. If explored in a careful manner, respecting the lives of the coral and any other sea creatures we encounter, these wonderful accumulations of life-forms will always be there for us to appreciate. But for this to happen, it is equally essential to strongly discourage destructive actions taken by other humans.

It seems inconceivable that anyone would deliberately harm such defenceless beauty. Isn't it enough that these poor reefs must contend with natural stresses, such as hurricanes, without adding the dangers of overfishing, pollution, exploitation, and tourism? In addition to being mined and blown apart to provide building materials, coral reefs are planted with explosives to blast out fish, whose dead or stunned bodies float to the surface for collection by fishermen. The limestone skeletons that form a large part of reefs are extracted to be used as fertilizer for mainland farming. Cruise ships strike tremendous blows when their anchors smash through delicate and millennia-old growths of coral. The tropical-fish industry has encouraged some individuals to bathe reefs in cyanide, to flush out delicately coloured fish. Repeated applications end up exterminating not only the fish but also the coral in which they had hidden. And, finally, sedimentation from deforestation blankets and suffocates fragile corals, which require clear water in which to live and breathe. Corals in areas throughout the world seem to be reacting to these incredible stresses by turning white. This bleaching process

The Great Barrier Reef, off the east coast of Australia, is the largest living structure visible from space and home to the greatest biodiversity of species in the sea.

Inset: The New Caledonian sea star lives in the shallow waters of lagoons.

precedes their death.

The Great Barrier Reef is now protected by the Great Barrier Reef Marine Park Act, passed by the Australian Parliament in 1975. Let's hope that more reefs in other areas of the world can also be protected in the future.

Slowly but surely, we are becoming more sensitized to the environment, not just in thought but in deed. Recognition of the importance of biodiversity to our continued presence on Earth is underscored by the recent signing of the United Nations Convention on Biodiversity by Canada in 1992 and the United States in 1993 after the World Summit on the Environment in Rio de Janeiro in 1992. And although not ratified by all countries, the Law of the Sea Convention is at least a recognition and open declaration by many countries that the oceans of the world must be protected. To be sure, acquiring new information and incorporating it into our economic and political policies requires a much longer time for some individuals than for others. Often this creates conflicts between environmentalists, who often see the issues with great urgency, and business people and politicians, who attempt to ensure a stable economic environment for their country within a complex global economy. In 1972, the first UN-sponsored international conference for the environment, The Stockholm Conference, was not supported either financially or politically because of such conflicts. However, twelve years later, when the discovery of the thinning of the ozone layer reached the popular press, politicians drafted the Montreal Protocol, bringing international pressure to ban the uses of chlorofluorocarbons (CFCs) by the year 2000.

Much-needed international cooperation on the environment has been encouraged by the wonderful development of a large assortment

Left: Pressing social and economic issues often prevent environmental concerns from being a top priority. Pollution from the industrial city of Troitsk, Russia, stains the white snows of the surrounding countryside.

Right: Air pollution from a cement plant in Africa.

of conservation and environmental groups. The establishment of nature reserves and marine parks has been due largely to the lobbying of politicians by such organizations and by concerned and usually very well-informed citizen groups or coalitions. Education and scientific research disseminate information that can improve human interaction with the ecosystem. In this regard we have come a long way since the publication of *The Silent Spring* by Rachel Carson in 1962. This book had a great influence on me when I was a teenager and books on the environment were few and far between. Today there is a plethora of calendars, books, and magazines with environmental themes. It is also heartening to find that, whereas in the past, the weather was the most popular topic of conversation between individuals who barely knew each other, today the environment is close to achieving the same status.

In the area of international cooperation, much can be done by industrialized countries in partnership with developing countries. They can help provide health and educational services, particularly to women who often suffer more than men from dwindling firewood and water supplies; women are often responsible for obtaining these vital resources and must travel long distances to locate them. Or they can extend environmental-protection policies to developing countries. Exploiting the natural resources of pristine environments while not practising state-of-the-art environmental protection that is mandatory at home is amoral.

In all countries, old legislation and policies that have not kept up with current thinking on the environment need to be updated. Activities that are detrimental to the environment, such as the use of carbon-rich fossil fuels, could be taxed, especially in areas where alternate forms of energy are viable. For example, it is estimated that South Dakota has enough wind energy to supply more than a quarter of the United States' electricity needs. In California, wind turbines already generate as much power as two large nuclear power plants. Activities that have positive economic and environmental effects, such as water reclaiming projects, could be charged lower taxes.

Many communities, with the encouragement of local and regional governments, have embarked upon active programs to set aside tin cans, bottles, plastic objects, and newspapers from their garbage for recycling. This may seem like a small step, but we don't have a magic wand to change the whole world overnight. It is very important for local communities to become involved in environmental matters, because any country is only as great as the smaller communities that form it. It is also crucial that the concerns of all members of the community are heard and not just those expressed by the most assertive voices. The !Kung people and San tribespeople have participated in the evolution of the natural ecosystem in Africa for many years, but with the introduction of technology and the extraordinary demands placed on their environment by cattle, even these adaptable people are not equipped to thrive. And in both Central and South America, native people who rely on the local environment for the continuation of a successful lifestyle, are endangered by outside pressures in which they have little or no voice.

In space, I was confident in the technology that provided me with the requirements of daily life — air, food, and water. But these space supplies completely depended upon the resources of the unique planet around which I orbited. I was not outside the world, but rather, still of the world. We usually cherish things that are unique. Why not the Earth?

FUTURE MISSIONS

HOW WILL FUTURE SPACE EXPLORERS FROM EARTH INTERACT WITH THE environment on another planet, particularly if we are unable to protect the one we have on our own world? Why should visiting the rainforests on Earth be any different from visiting unique areas on another planet? Will economic and political pressures adversely affect our relationship with any new life-form that we may encounter? Personally, I would feel more confident in our ability to explore and live on another planet in a reasonable, sustainable manner if we were doing the same on Earth.

In 1977, the space probes *Voyager 1* and *2* were sent on a mission to explore other planets, and then to carry on into deep space. Onboard, there is a recording of various sounds of the Earth. Whales'

In 1981, twenty-seven of these dish-shaped antennae in New Mexico began to receive radio waves emitted by objects in the depths of space. The signals are analyzed by computers to produce exciting details of faraway galaxies.

voices, children laughing, and music await discovery, somewhere, sometime. They will travel farther than any feature of *Homo sapiens* has ever travelled. What is significant about the recording is that it reflects not our ability to make war or exploit the Earth's natural resources, but our wish to reveal the real beauty of our world and each other. *Homo sapiens*, at least in the *Voyager* recording, seems to be a responsible, benevolent, sharing species. Wouldn't it be great if we could learn to live up to our advance billing before some other life-form pays us a visit in response to our invitation, or before we go exploring ourselves?

Like the *Apollo* missions to the moon, future space missions will need to chart, map, observe, and annotate the environment of a new planet before a landing is made. I use the word "environment" deliberately, because in the past we have thought of new worlds in a geophysical sense and ignored the complex interactions between living and nonliving elements. We need to know beforehand what the environmental consequences of landing or walking on another planet for the first time will be. The fact that there would be few human beings initially will delay the cumulative effects of too many people in one place. On Earth, we are still trying to define terrestrial life-support systems and human effects upon them. On other planets, there may be an even more delicate balance to maintain. Although there has been a great latitude in the acceptance of people by other life-forms on our planet, this may not be the case elsewhere. Collecting and displacing any object or organism may have long-range effects.

The 250-million-year-old Carlsbad Caverns in New Mexico, which were devoid of human life before the early explorers visited them, are an example of an environment that has been altered by contact with humans. The caverns are now a tourist attraction, and the minute flakes of skin and body oils people leave behind attract a "cleanup crew" of crickets. If food wasn't prohibited by park rangers, larger animals might enter the caverns to feed on leftovers. One can only guess at the cycle that might follow, with people pressed to defend the territory in the caves from the "intruders."

It is difficult to believe that we would do something deliberately to curtail or preclude the life span of a species on a new planet, but we have frequently taken this step on our own planet. No doubt we should think of this with respect to Earth before travelling elsewhere in space, and not make excuses that it is too late to change attitudes or living styles.

Future space habitations will use a closed environmental life-support system. All the life-forms in this type of system depend upon one another to cycle food, water, and air without relying on the outside environment. When agriculture was first practised on Earth, the small population could participate in such a cycle quite successfully. The size of the resource base was immense compared to the number of humans interacting with it. We still live in a closed environmental life-support system on Earth with an infusion of energy from the sun. However, our population of billions has forced upon this closed system activities for which it was not designed to cope with naturally. If we change our environmental life-support system too drastically, we may change it in a direction that may not allow us, even with our technology, to deal with the consequences. Before we live in a closed system on another planet, we need to consider the one we already are part of here on Earth.

Although we may want to venture out into the solar system to explore other planetary bodies, at the moment we are hampered by our inefficiency at travelling even short distances. We may have reached the moon, but access to that extraterrestrial world is very much Earthbound. The gallant "sailing ships" of the *Apollo* missions of the late 1960s and early 1970s now grace the halls of museums. The drive to reignite our exploration of outer space is currently an international effort, with formerly feuding space-faring nations now combining their experience and resources to achieve new heights and embrace new worlds. The shuttle's success has proven that human beings can, in short periods, access the microgravity environment around low Earth orbit. The powerful rockets developed in the former Soviet Union continue to carry wave after wave of Russian cosmonauts to inhabit the MIR space station for much longer periods than the shuttle can accommodate.

A revolutionary single-stage rocket design is a promising new mode of access to the world above Earth's atmosphere. Using state-of-the-art composite materials, such as epoxy and graphite fibres, the Delta Clipper launches vertically and rotates to descend to the Earth in a vertical configuration, after two days in orbit, with two additional days in reserve. It appear to be safer, more versatile, and cheaper than current spaceships.

Looking beyond low Earth orbit and the friendly moon, many of the planets that are sometimes mistaken in the night sky for bright, shining stars have haunted people throughout the ages as places of mystery and romance. Venus does not appear to be any closer from the shuttle than it does from Earth. It still looks like an evening star. The 100 million km (62 million mi.) average distance of Venus from

Earth seemed to shrink considerably when the *Mariner 10* unmanned spacecraft approached Venus in February 1974 to a distance of 5310 km (3,300 mi.), dispelling forever the myth that the second planet in our solar system is Earth's twin. The surface temperature of 482° C (900° F) and an atmospheric pressure ninety times that of Earth's ended any discussion of a manned exploration of Venus.

Mars, on the other hand, is very much on the minds of scientists and astronauts. Ever since Galileo first laid a telescopic eye on this planet, around the year 1610, it has conjured up theories of extraterrestrials and advanced civilizations. When I first entered the world of science fiction, many years ago, I memorized artists' descriptions of the surface of Mars. These included beautiful canal systems, described in the 1860s by astronomer Pietro Angelo Secchi as faint, linear features on the surface of the red planet. Percival Lowell later postulated that an advanced civilization had built extensive canal systems and, furthermore, had outlawed war! Around the same time, in the early 1900s, better telescopes and photographs failed to confirm the canals' existence. When the Earth passes between Mars and the sun, the two planets may be separated by 55 million km (34 million mi.), but when they are on opposites sides of the sun, the distance expands to 400 million km (249 million mi.). At this distant point, the surface features of Mars cannot be distinguished with Earth telescopes.

Mariner 4 changed all this on July 15, 1965, when close-up photographs of the surface from about 3000 m (9,843 ft.) above it revealed a cratered area resembling those of the lunar highlands. The most historic mission to Mars occurred on July 20, 1976, when the first *Viking* lander, *Viking 1*, touched down on the planet. *Viking 2* landed at a different site on September 3, 1976. These spacecraft monitored the Martian environment for almost two full Martian years, which is 1,374 Earth days. They discovered that Mars has a thin atmosphere, with low surface pressures, a very small magnetic field, and cold temperatures ranging from –69° C (–92° F) just before dawn to –25° C (–13° F) by mid-afternoon. They also acquired information on the comings and goings of global dust storms, the changing distribution of fine-grained material on the surface, and dynamic weather patterns and polar ice caps.

Mars has captured the imagination of space explorers for many years. Although it may seem like science fiction, the entire surface has already been mapped in preparation for a possible manned landing. Mars is a seemingly quiet world despite volcanoes that dwarf any on the face of our Earth. Mars' Olympus Mons, the largest known volcano in the solar system, is 24 km (15 mi.) high and more than 480 km (300 mi.) across its base, whereas Mauna Loa, Earth's largest, rises only 10 km (6 mi.) above the ocean floor. Before exposing astronauts to an inhospitable environment, scientists are striving to understand the rates of meteoric impact, crater formation, and volcanic eruptions which on Mars last for years. The different composition of the Martian atmosphere at the surface, known to be 95.3 percent carbon dioxide, 2.7 percent nitrogen,

Left: This computer-reconstructed view of Mars is similar to one that would be taken from a spacecraft at a distance of 2000 km (1,240 mi.) from the surface. The large dark mark, which is called Syrtis Major, appears to be volcanic in origin.

Right: For seven years after landing on the surface of Mars in 1976, the two Viking spacecraft relayed information back to Earth. Small trenches in the centre foreground of this photograph were dug by a lander's soil-sampler arm.

and 1.6 percent argon, with oxygen at a rare 0.13 percent, means that supplemental life-support systems will be worn by all intrepid Earthlings who explore Mars.

One question scientists sought to answer from data extracted from the *Viking* landers was whether or not any life-forms exist in the Martian soil. Initially, there was great excitement, with the discovery of possible vegetative materials that suggested life. But recalibration of the *Viking* lander's equipment eventually led to a declaration that the surface of Mars is devoid of life. Recently, however, some scientists involved in the original *Viking* missions have opened up these conclusions to question, based on a reconsideration of the sensitivity and calibration of the equipment.

The mysterious Martian planet will continue to be the object of space exploration efforts. The first "footprints" on Mars were made by the *Viking1* lander, but perhaps within the lifetime of many of us, another set of footprints will be made by humans. It is more difficult to conceive of a trip farther away, from where we will no longer be able to see our precious Earth. Encountering the large gaseous planets of the outer solar system, in sizes that cannot be imagined, is particularly hard to comprehend. *Voyager 1* and *Voyager 2* entered the Jovian system in March and July 1979, beaming back astounding images of the planet Jupiter, which is 778 million km (483 million mi.) away from Earth. This immense planet has a diameter eleven times that of Earth. Its giant red spot, a great storm system that has been observed for almost three hundred years, would swallow three planets the size of ours. How will a human being grasp the immensity of such a sight when the Earth is great only in memory? It will be an awesome experience, one filled no doubt with fear and apprehension.

In our future missions, we may encounter many unusual land-forms and life-forms that are totally unknown to us at this time. On the return home, glimpsing the beautiful, complex rings of Saturn, or the methane gases of Neptune, will evoke a deep feeling of relief that the home planet, Earth, is near. The richness of Earth is not, as far as we know, duplicated elsewhere in the solar system. Although it is naive to think that our planet boasts the only life-forms in space, we should recognize that as far as the eye can see, there is no one quite like us.

Left above: This image of Jupiter taken by Voyager 2 includes the area from Jupiter's equator to the southern polar region near the Great Red Spot, which is the size of three Earths. One of Jupiter's moons, Io, passes by the northern edge of the Great Red Spot, while another, Europa, passes above one of the many white ovals on the planet that were first noticed more than fifty years ago.

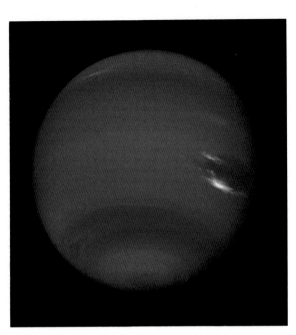

We listen for signs of others in deep space. We search the world overhead, and around us, for answers to why we are here. As we leave the surface of our planet for other far-distant worlds, we should never forget our roots and our life-support system that has made us who we are today.

I am of the Earth, and as I orbited the Earth, I felt secure knowing that this beautiful, evolving sphere was my home planet. As I touched the world with my eyes and with cameras from space, I felt that I could touch the landscape below. But I couldn't. It is only here, on the surface of this great, glowing blue world, that I can touch the Earth. And when I do, it is with reverence and awe.

GLOSSARY

A/G	Air to ground		NTD	NASA test director
CDR	Commander		OMS	Orbital maneuvering system
DTO	Detailed technical objective		OTC	Orbiter test conductor
ET	External tank		RSO	Range safety officer
Field Mill	Measures static discharge in the local atmosphere		SRB	Solid rocket booster
GLS	Ground launch sequencer		STS-42	Space Transportation System flight number 42
GMT	Greenwich Mean Time		ZULU	Greenwich Mean Time
MECO	Main engine cut off			

SELECT BIBLIOGRAPHY

Allaby, A., and M. Allaby, eds. *The Concise Oxford Dictionary of Earth Sciences.* New York: Oxford University Press, 1990.

Allan, T., and A. Warren, eds. *Deserts: The Encroaching Wilderness.* New York: Oxford University Press, 1993.

Bailey, R.H. *Planet Earth Glacier.* Alexandria, Va.: Time-Life, 1982.

Bondar, B.C., with R.L. Bondar. *On the Shuttle.* Toronto: Greey de Pencier, 1993.

Brown, B., and L. Morgan. *The Miracle Planet.* New York: Gallery Books, 1990.

Cannon, L., and M. Goyen. *Exploring Australia's Great Barrier Reef.* Australia: Watermark Press, 1990.

Carr, M.H. *The Surface of Mars.* New Haven, Conn.: Yale University Press, 1981.

Chronic, H. *Roadside Geology of New Mexico.* Missoula, Mont.: Mountain Press Publishing Company, 1987.

Cousteau, J. *The Ocean World.* New York: Harry N. Abrams, 1985.

Cribb, J. *Subtidal Galapagos.* Buffalo, N.Y.: Camden House, 1986.

Darwin, C. *The Structure and Distribution of Coral Reefs.* 2d ed. London: Smith, Elder and Company, 1874.

Dickinson, T. *From the Big Bang to Planet X.* Buffalo, N.Y.: Camden House, 1993.

Forsyth, A., and K. Miyata. *Tropical Nature.* New York: Charles Scribner's Sons, 1984.

Frith, C., and D. Frith. *Australian Tropical Reef Life.* Townsville, Australia: Tropical Australia Graphics, 1987.

Gouldsmith, E., N. Hildyard, P. McCully, and P. Bunyard. *Imperiled Planet.* Cambridge: MIT Press, 1990.

Harris, M. *A Field Guide to the Birds of Galapagos.* Toronto: HarperCollins, 1982.

Kingdon, J. *Island Africa.* Princeton, N.J.: Princeton University Press, 1989.

Larsen, P. *The Deserts of the Southwest: A Sierra Club Naturalists Guide.* San Francisco: Sierra Club Books, 1977.

Levine, J.L. and J. Rotman. *The Coral Reef at Night.* New York: Harry N. Abrams, 1993.

MacInnis, J., ed. *Saving the Oceans.* Toronto: Key Porter Books, 1992.

Main, M. *Kalahari.* Johannesburg: Southern Book Publishers, 1977.

Marx, W. *The Fragile Ocean.* Old Saybrook, Conn.: The Globe Pequot Press, 1991.

Mungall, C., and D.J. McLaren, eds. *Planet Under Stress: The Challenge of Global Change.* Toronto: Oxford University Press, 1991.

Ross, Karen. *Jewel of the Kalahari: Okavango.* London: BBC Books, 1992.

Silcock, L., ed. *The Rainforests, A Celebration.* San Francisco: Chronicle Books, 1992.

Skinner, B.J., and S.C. Porter. *The Dynamic Earth.* New York: John Wiley and Sons, 1989.

Tablot, F.H., and R.E. Stevenson, eds. *Encyclopedia of the Earth, Oceans, and Islands.* London: Murehurst, 1991.

Van Rose, S., and I.F. Mercer. *Volcanos.* Cambridge: Harvard University Press, 1991.

World Resources, 1992-1993. New York: Oxford University Press, 1992.

World Resources Institute. *1994 Information Please — Environmental Almanac.* New York: Houghton Mifflin, 1993.

Worldwatch. *State of the World, 1993.* New York: W.W. Norton, 1993.

INDEX

Numbers in italics refer to photographs.